TOM CLAN

Preaching the Word

REFLECTIONS ON THE GOSPELS
OF THE THREE-YEAR CYCLE

THE COLUMBA PRESS
DUBLIN 1992

First edition, 1992, published by
THE COLUMBA PRESS
93, The Rise, Mount Merrion, Blackrock, Co Dublin.

Cover by Bill Bolger
Origination by The Columba Press
Printed in Ireland by
Colour Books, Dublin.

ISBN 1 85607 029 8

Contents

YEAR A

YEAR B

YEAR C

Preface

Since August 1978, I have been writing reflections regularly for the *Cork Examiner*. One group of these reflections relates to the Sunday readings; others arise from current events or themes.

From those relating to the readings, I have selected one for each Sunday and some other occasions in the three year cycle. In most cases I have written on particular readings several times over the fourteen years. I have confined this selection to reflections on the gospel of the day.

Many readers and friends have encouraged me to continue the ongoing newspaper contributions and helped me in compiling this selection. I am very grateful to each one of them.

My personal thanks to Fergus O' Callaghan, Editor, *Cork Examiner* and to his colleagues for facilitating the venture and for their competent and kind co-operation always.

My thanks to Seán O Boyle and the staff at The Columba Press whose interest and commitment made the production of this book a very worthwhile experience for me. I hope you enjoy the fruit of our work and are enriched in some way through it.

Tom Clancy

Year A

First Sunday of Advent

Mt 24:37-44

The bare trees and the long dark evenings speak of year's end. In the world of nature, life seems almost totally dormant with little sign of anything to look forward to. In contrast, on the commercial scene, the pace quickens everyday with so few shopping days left to Christmas that we need to be up and doing. The opportunity for bargains could slip by. This chance will not come again. Hurry, be ready, spend, choose and be wise. There is an urgency in the advertisers' message. Prepare to celebrate.

As we hear this weekend, the Advent message has the same urgency, the clarion call to readiness. The same language is used but the focus is different. The commercial focus is on things and more things and the more expensive the better. The Christian focus is on persons and relationships. The reminder is that the forthcoming festival is an anniversary of God's sending his Son among us to bind us together as one family.

We best prepare for this feast by strengthening our relationships with one another and with God. To be a first mover in forgiveness will be a good start. To bridge a grudge, to reach out in hope and love to somebody from whom we are alienated, even a little, will be a superb step in readying ourselves for the festival. Reconciliation cannot happen unless somebody takes the first step. Advent is a time when God enables each of us to take it, so preparing for the coming of the Lord. Hurry and be ready.

Second Sunday of Advent

Mt 3:1-12

To live without hope is the greatest human poverty. For many who live even in the midst of the greatest hardship, the ray of hope is kept alive by the love of those around them and by the love of God they experience through their neighbours. On the other hand, some who are so wealthy that their Christmas present will be the one advertised 'for the person who has everything,' live in prisons of despair without hope in anyone, least of all in themselves. In between, there is an endless rainbow of hopes and despairs in all our hearts. On the world canvas, there is so little to be hopeful about. Why hope?

We hope because of God's promises and their fulfilment. As we hear on Sunday, he promised to send a saviour and he sent his Son. The Son promised that the Spirit of God would make a home in our hearts enabling us to share friendship with God in a way that enables us to grow in loving service to each other. This is the reason for our hope. Recognising his presence in others, responding to it in so many ways, keeps hope alive. A person of hope lives forever. One without hope dies a thousand deaths each day.

Sunday's gospel challenges us to prepare a way for the Lord by keeping hope alive in our world today.

Third Sunday of Advent

Mt 11:2-11

Having reprimanded the local ruler for his immoral lifestyle, John the Baptist ended up in prison with plenty of time to think. He wondered whether his cousin really was the promised saviour after all. John had expected a more militant type. So, he sent a pal to ask Jesus the straight question. The reply was blunt. 'You know what I am doing, the blind see again, the deaf have their hearing restored and the poor are being given new hope. Judge for yourself.' John believed him.

Today, in the midst of many options and choices, imprisoned by anxieties and uncertainties, bombarded by a variety of claimants for their allegiance, the young especially, and the not so young, too, ask a similar question of the Church. Are you the promised saviour of the world?

The question is addressed to each of us, leaders and people. No answer in mere words will satisfy. In our time, service is more persuasive than doctrine. The young are more influenced by lifestyle than by preaching or teaching. Do our actions bring hope to the poor? Maybe our prayers today should ask God to remove our blindness to enable us to see the plight of the alienated, to open our ears to the cry of the poor.

Are you the ones who are to come or do we look for another? It is a challenging question for each of us.

Fourth Sunday of Advent
Mt 1:18-24

Broken contracts lead to disharmony and violence. The person who does not keep a promise creates ever-widening ripples of distrust. The unfulfilled pledge is a wound that wrankles unceasingly. To break one's word to a child is to undermine confidence that may never be restored. On the other hand, a commitment honoured, a vow kept, a covenant fulfilled creates bonds of peace and love that can survive any calamity.

Today's Mass reminds us of one such promise. The promise in question was God's, to send a saviour, a rescuer, a leader. He sent his own Son, Jesus born of Mary, a Jew of the line of David who would rise from the dead to enable us to believe in God and in our destiny. He gave his word to be our God no matter how we failed. To seal that promise his Son took flesh and continues to live amongst us as a builder of peace based on justice.

God continues to keep his word. Today is another invitation to respond in faith-filled joy and generous fidelity.

Christmas Day

Lk 2:1-14

There was a howling November storm blowing when the man of the roads turned in through the familiar gates sure of a welcome and a warm meal. His hopes were well founded because he had never been turned away from this house. His expectations were met once more. But by the time it came to his leaving, the weather had worsened and the family insisted that he should stay the night with them.

A mattress was placed before the kitchen fire to ensure his comfort. Next day the weather was no better so he stayed another night and eventually, he stayed the rest of the winter. After that, for the rest of his life, he came off the roads each November and spent the winter with these caring friends. When he died they buried him in their own family plot.

People thought them foolish. He might have burned the house down with his cigarette butts. Others wondered were the children at risk from assault or disease. Besides, he might be a thief. Anyway, why did they open their home to this stranger? There was nothing in it for them. Many considered that it was going too far with kindness. But love does such things.

Some years before a young girl and her husband did not find such a welcome where they had called and she gave birth to her son in a cave stable. It was a poor start to a life that had its share of suffering and rejection and which ended with crucifixion as a criminal. Many nodded their heads at the foolishness of Mary's son.

The learned were puzzled and still are, that an all-knowing God would allow this to happen to the only Son. He knew the risks. Was it not going a bit too far? Surely there must have been another way to establish his kingdom on earth? Why was he not born a

14

prince or, at least, in the centre of things rather than in Bethlehem? If he were to be a great leader his education would have been better even in Jerusalem rather than in the back of beyond called Nazareth. Even to win men's hearts it was going too far, many thought and think. But love does such things.

May each of our needy brothers and sisters have a haven of love to turn into off the roadway of life when the howling storm of poverty, unemployment, homelessness or discouragement whirl around them now or in the year ahead. May Christ turn into each of our hearts and homes this Christmas and in the New Year.

Happy Christmas.

Holy Family
Mt 2:13-15, 19-23

We so often picture Jesus as working miracles, instructing the disciples, standing up to the Scribes, dying on Calvary, that we may forget that like us, he had to grow from the security of childhood, through the uncertainty of adolescence into the maturity of adulthood. While his growth may have been more sure-footed than most, his search and learning were as gradual as our own. He learned Joseph's trade. Like any other mother, Mary cared for him while wondering what her child would turn out to be. Like any child, he was greatly formed by the adults in his life and, in turn, they were enriched by his presence. His relationship within the family moulded him and blessed the parents. In so many ways, it was just like any child growing up in a family.

The feast of the Holy Family is a reminder of how precious and central family is at all stages of one's life. Like every family, the family at Nazareth had its own unique and not quite normal story. They were homeless when the child was born. They were forced to emigrate. On their return, they had some happy years until the man of the house died. Shortly afterwards, the Son left the family business and went about making his own life which ended in seeming disaster on a cross, condemned as a criminal. In that family story, God's plan was accomplished.

Something similar is true of every family story. It is in a family situation that God's plan is worked out most of the time. Today is an opportunity to reflect on our own situation.

Maybe, like the family of Nazareth, we need each other to be more fully present to each other and for each other in the year ahead. Precious things always need to be protected and nurtured.

Second Sunday of Christmas

Eph 1:3-6, 15-18

Jn 1:1-18

Christmas is special in a home where there is a young baby, more particularly, if it is the first-born of the family. Somehow, the infant's presence puts us in tune with the feelings of joy and happiness that were in Mary's and Joseph's hearts on the first Christmas night. Their excitement about his safe delivery, his obvious good health, every whimper and movement of Mary's boy must have so engrossed them that they could almost have forgotten who Jesus really was, the Son of God as well as the son of Mary. Focused, as we are at this time, on the crib in Bethlehem and on the wise men, we too need to be reminded that Mary's son is divine. Today's Mass alerts us to what we believe. Paul and John, two great exponents of the good news, put the message before us, each in his own way. Paul's enthusiastic hymn of praise emphasises that all we have received from God comes to us through Christ, the chosen one of the Father, and Paul prays for us that we can gradually become more and more aware of what hope God's call has in store for us. On the other hand, John's gospel hymn is more reflective and austere. He highlights that the one born of the virgin is the eternal creator of all that there is, who comes among us as a light to guide us on our way through life to final happiness with God.

Between them, Paul and John realign us for the year ahead with the essentials of our faith. We will do well to heed them.

Epiphany
Mt 2:1-12

There are people who have a very clear goal in life and all their energies are directed towards it. It may be money, friendship with God, political power, family happiness, prestige, success in sport or a top job. Whatever it is, it is like a single star that beckons them onwards relentlessly and strengthens them to endure every inconvenience and sacrifice that is needed to attain it.

In today's gospel, we read of the wise men from the east who followed their single star and it led them to Jesus. They could have stayed where they were but instead they paid the price of long journeying and of risking their lives by approaching Herod. Their reward was the opportunity to meet Jesus and to worship him as their God.

Unlike those famous travellers, most of us are less definite about what we want out of life. We follow many little stars, a bit of comfort and security as well as small selfishnesses here and there. We can be like Herod and expect somebody else to find Jesus for us. It cannot be done. We must be prepared to pay the price of time and service to meet him. The world today offers as many beckoning stars as the myriad of stars in the Milky Way. Each person must choose one rather than the rest.

Which star are you following this year?

Baptism of the Lord

Mt 3:13-17

Giving in to another is often seen as a sign of weakness. When a government gives in to a pressure group or a parent to a tantrum child in the supermarket, the response is due to unfair pressure. But people give in on other occasions. A loved one may give in to the pleas of the beloved just to share the joy it brings. In today's gospel, we find John the Baptist, the austere, disciplined, strong-willed prophet giving in to his cousin from Nazareth and baptising Jesus as he demanded. Why did such a determined man as the Baptist give in? He must have realised that Jesus was special and that to do whatever Jesus wants is always best even if we do not fully understand the reason for his request. Sometimes, we are quite aware of Jesus' requests to us. It may be to heal a quarrel, to let a grievance go, to make our peace with God, to give up the drink, to serve our neighbour in a new way, maybe even to give our lives fully to him in priesthood or religious life. He never exerts undue pressure but we know in the depth of our being what he wants of us, but will not give in. Why? Perhaps, we do not trust him to know what is best. Maybe the price is too high or we are too self-willed to heed his call, which often comes to us in the ordinary circumstances of life.

Today is an invitation to give in to Jesus as the Baptist did, no matter what he asks.

Ash Wednesday

Mt 6:1-6, 16-18

The greatest threat to love is forgetfulness. We forget the gift of friendship and focus on what we have given in a relationship. In moments of selfishness we calculate that we have done more than enough to earn a better response than we are getting. Then we withdraw into ourselves, protecting ourselves from the pains of sharing and live in the barrenness of isolation which rapidly crushes the human spirit in our hearts. We forget that we owe even our very existence to a sharing of others and of God himself – a giving beyond all hope of recompense. Sharing can be a deliberate investment with guaranteed returns or it can be the generous outpouring of the goodness of the giver. True friendship, human or divine, belongs to the latter category.

To forget such friendship is to die to part of oneself. Lent is an antidote to such forgetfulness. It reminds us of how God gives himself to us everyday and enables us to give to one another in joy and peace. The sacrifices of Lent are not only to curb selfishness but to open our hearts to the joy of being loved by God and by each other more deeply once again. Lent is for friendship. It is an opportunity not to be missed.

First Sunday of Lent

Mt 4:1-11

Human nature is the same the world over. Each generation has persons of outstanding courage like Archbishop Romero, of great service like Mother Teresa and of supreme generosity like Maximillian Kolbe. Yet the same human nature which is often capable of such strength is also open to temptation. The temptation is to use other people and one's own gifts for totally selfish purposes. In varied disguises, the same temptation comes to each person again and again in life. What makes some people different is the choice they make in such situations.

Being human, Jesus was tempted. For him, the crunch was whether to use his power as Son of God for his own satisfaction and for glory from men. As we hear in the gospel, he chose instead to follow the Father's plan and to give his life in service of others.

Today, the temptation for many is to misuse their position, talent or wealth for their own benefit to the detriment of the weak, the ordinary, the less well off. The easy justification is the blasé opinion that what I have is mine and that is how the world is. Yes, but it is not how the Father wants the world to be. In big things and small, we are asked to surrender privilege, power and popularity so that others may have food, freedom and friendship in decency and dignity.

There is no end to what one person's courageous and generous choices can achieve be it Jesus, Niall O'Brien, Helen Keller or just, you and I.

Second Sunday of Lent

Mt 17: 1-9

Killarney's Torc Waterfall, in full spate after the unprecedented heavy rainfall, brought out the sightseers. One Sunday afternoon as hardy souls climbed the slope, the weather broke and lightning flashed across the sky. Even the bravest scurried for shelter and for home. To enjoy the wonder of creation in the cascading torrent and sparkling spray was invigorating and very safe. To experience lightning on the exposed mountainside was eerie and frightening. But even in that momentary fear, there was a new insight into the glory of God's creation, an insight not to be repeated, perhaps, but to be remembered always. It was an enrichment only for those who had ventured forth from the comfort and security of home.

When Jesus took Peter, James and John to Mount Tabor, they glimpsed not just the glory of God's creation but the very nature of God himself. Jesus forbade them to tell the others about it because it could not begin to be understood until he was risen from the dead when the disciples began to realise who he really was.

Great Tabor experiences do not come often in any of our lives, but even mini-Tabors cannot come our way unless we venture to explore the mystery of God in creation and in his friendship in prayer. Today's gospel is a reminder never to put limits on what God can enable us to become.

Third Sunday of Lent

Jn 4:5-42

Today's gospel is one of the unforgetable incidents in Christ's life. Nothing should distract us from its impact. Indeed, to get its full flavour it could be read by a team of readers, one for the narrative, one for the Samaritan woman and one for Jesus' part. The setting is perfect. Jesus, dying with the thirst at a well over a hundred feet deep, has no bucket. The outcast, the Samaritan woman, has a bucket and a rope, presumably. The stage is set for stubborn confrontation or face-saving bargaining. Jesus chooses neither of these alternatives. Instead, he uses his own need of drinking water to awaken in the woman an awareness of her need of God. He succeeds not only in her case, but in the case of her townspeople as well.

It is a power-filled story. Conscious as we all are of our need for food and drink, this gospel incident alerts us to reflect on our need for God, our need to let his life of grace nourish our faith, hope and love so that eternal life will flourish within us. Otherwise, his presence among us can be parched to death.

Fourth Sunday of Lent

Jn 9:1-41

To help me remember which way the clock changes, a man told me once that it springs forward an hour in the spring and falls back in the fall. It means that in spring we lose an hour's daylight in the morning and gain it in the evening. It is very noticeable for a week or so after the time changes, noticeable for those who can see the dawn and appreciate the sunset. It is a change that the blind do not appreciate in the same way.

Daylight for the blind is still darkness. To be born blind is a thought that frightens most people so much that many tend to shirk meeting those so afflicted. Jesus met one such man and confronted the difficulty head on. He cured the man.

John recounts it in today's gospel as one of the seven great signs that Jesus worked so that people might believe in him as Son of God. True enough, the man was cured and that was a blessing beyond compare. But there was more to it than that. Jesus introduced him not only to daylight but to faith, not only to be able to see the wonders of the ordinary everyday world but also to recognise in faith the presence of God around him. This is an ability that we all need, to be able to see God's hand in our lives. The darkness of selfishness blocks our seeing Christ in our brother in need and our recognising God's will when he calls us to be heroic in living out our baptismal privileges. It is our blindness that only Jesus can remove. Today is a day to ask the Lord to restore our vision of our greatness as followers of his and give us the courage like the man in the gospel to proclaim to one and all that Jesus of Nazareth is the great prophet, the Son of God to whom we give our allegiance.

Fifth Sunday of Lent

Jn 11:1-45

Last week's gospel told how Jesus cured the man born blind. This weekend, he goes one better. He raises a dead man to life. What must have been Martha's thoughts as she saw the master stand before the grave in which her brother had been buried for four days and call out his name in a loud voice. 'Lazarus, come out!'? She could well have felt that Jesus must be cracking up under the grief of losing his good friend. After such a long time, there could now be no way in which Lazarus could come back. But come back he did. Surely this Jesus must be very special, one whose call could be heard and answered no matter what the obstacle, even through death itself.

This weekend, Jesus calls us again to come out of the tomb of our selfishness. Maybe we feel we are too settled to change. We have been so long in the grave of our mediocrity and sin that we could not possibly expect to respond. It was not his own strength that enabled Lazarus to return to life but the power of God. It is this same power that calls us and enables us to break out of the fetters of fear-filled self-centredness to serve our neighbour and our God in a new life of generous love. Now is an opportunity for us to hear his call and to receive his power to be changed to a better life.

Passion Sunday

Mt 26:14 – 27:66

Thirty pieces of silver. It was a tidy sum and easy to come by. All he had to do was to lead the Jewish guards to where Jesus was spending the night. Judas reassured himself that he was not doing anything illegal. In fact, he had the law on his side. Anyway, if Jesus were as powerful as he claimed to be, he should be well able to look after himself. If he were not, then he was an impostor and should be removed for the common good. Besides, the authorities would arrest him eventually so he might as well have the thirty pieces of silver as anybody else.

All in all, Judas reasoned, you have to take your chances, to get on in life. He would look after himself and let the others do the same. One cannot look after everybody. There was a niggling doubt that betraying a man was wrong but Judas quickly smothered that thought. He made his choice. He probably did not foresee all the consequences of his actions and, as we read in today's gospel, his regret-filled suicide did nothing to undo the damage he had caused.

Many of us have Judas' moments in our lives.

Good Friday

Jn 18:1 – 19:42

To be deserted by a friend in time of need is always a crippling blow. To be deserted by one's committed life partner can be devastating beyond measure. On Good Friday, Jesus felt the pain of both experiences.

When the going got tough, even the closest disciples ran for cover with Peter cursing and denying that he ever knew the man. But worse still for Jesus, he felt deserted even by his Father, as the agony deepened. The prayer wrung from his desperate heart was 'My God, my God, why have you forsaken me?' It is the prayer of all who suffer – the sick, the bereaved, the wronged and the failures.

Like Jesus, many will feel that God has distanced himself from them and nothing seems left but a death like Calvary. There is no denying the suffering and pain of human living and dying. These are real and must be faced and accepted. But just as Calvary was not the end for Jesus, neither is suffering the end for us. There is hope.

The week's celebration of the death and resurrection is an opportunity to experience the fidelity of our God who never deserts us, but comes to us again and again in reconciliation and eucharist and constantly through the love of the community among whom we live and work and spend our lives. It is an opportunity not to be missed.

27

Holy Saturday

Mt 28:1-10

On Sunday last I saw a swallow for the first time this year. He swooped almost to ground level, drawing my attention to the green blades peeping through the soil, and then he soared again into the sunshine. The movement was beautiful. It was good to be alive. Then, quite unexpectedly, the weather turned cold. Almost without notice, giant hailstones showered down all around, shattering my illusion that the summer was here. Yet, the memory of the swallow lifted my heart. Winter must be over. The swallow does not bring the summer but he is a sign and a reminder of its coming. His arrival awakens hope and creates anticipation.

For me, the paschal candle is like that swallow. It is a symbol of the Risen Christ's presence among us. It draws our attention to the new life he brings us. It is a reminder that the Christ who suffered for us is now alive and present to us through his Church. In times of doubt and suffering, the memory of Christ's resurrection sustains us. It is because we are called to eternal life with him that we can love and serve the neighbour, above and beyond the call of duty. Christ's resurrection is the keel of our faith, the key to our hope and the kernel of our love.

Happy resurrection days to you.

Easter Sunday

Jn 20:1-9

Many people have stood by an open grave and wondered whether this is the end of all. Is everything over for the deceased? Certainly when Jesus died, the disciples thought it was all over for him and their own future looked pretty bleak as well. They had seen the miracles and everything else he had done. Indeed, they were so captivated by his achievements that they failed even to glimpse the person behind them, the one who was loved so fully by the Father in the Holy Spirit from all eternity and for all eternity. It was only through the gift of the Holy Spirit after the resurrection that the disciples came to recognise the person of Jesus who would live among us forever.

This is the core of our faith. We are more than our accomplishments, our possessions or our reputations. After death, these become irrelevant anyway. The only thing that lasts is love. The essence of who we are is that we are unique individuals loved by God. When God loves, it must be forever. In him, there is no change. So whatever happens at death our identity remains the same, we are God's chosen ones.

On the first Easter day, the same Jesus who was crucified, but is now transformed by the Holy Spirit, returned to his mother and to the disciples, to show them and us that he would live forever in the bosom of the father, and that same destiny awaits us. The Easter gift is to believe in the transforming power of the Holy Spirit so that we can grow in the belief that each one of us is the Beloved of God who will love us forever in a way that is totally beyond our understanding just now, but which is the cornerstone of inner peace and indeed, of world peace. Lord, increase our faith.

Happy Easter.

Second Sunday of Easter

Jn 20:19-31

Selfish and self-righteous bargaining is a strong strand in our human condition. It often shows itself in the 'unless' syndrome. It can start early in life. The young owner of a football will not let the others play unless he is centre-forward. He can maintain this attitude even though he is dependent on the others for a game. Sometimes this leads to everybody losing out.

The 'unless' syndrome often strengthens with age and becomes a diseased attitude which permeates both industrial relations, under the respectable guise of hard bargaining, and family relationships under the pretext of protecting future harmony. 'I will not unless you...' can sound so reasonable but it usually shows an inability or unwillingness to trust another. Often this view can be justified but in other situations the 'unless' approach is no substitute for trust.

Today's gospel has the story of one such situation. Having missed the visit of the Risen Lord, Thomas rants that he will not believe unless certain conditions are met. In his great love the Lord meets these conditions to enable the doubting Thomas to believe. But more is promised to those who believe and trust unconditionally, who trust God and others.

To be able to trust is a marvellous gift to be prayed for constantly. To be willing to trust is a decision that one can chose to make or not. Our decisions gradually make us what we become. Only the Spirit can ensure that the 'unless' syndrome does not wreck our relationships with one another and with God.

Third Sunday of Easter

Lk 24:13-35

It is a sobering thought that one could meet the risen Lord and not recognise him. As we read in today's gospel, it happened to two disciples on the road to Emmaus. Having spent years in his company, they knew him well and had banked on him to come up trumps. Instead, he had died on a cross betraying all their hopes. Even though the word was out that he had risen, they left town in a hurry afraid to hope in him again. He joined them on the road and they did not recognise him until they shared their home and their food with him. Then they recognised him in the breaking of bread.

Many of us have spent years in his company and service. We can lose hope in him. The world does not seem to have changed because of our prayers. He does not seem to have lifted our burdens, perhaps. Some may feel that he has betrayed their hopes. We may be afraid to place our hopes in him again, afraid to risk the foolhardiness of total commitment to him as Lord. We want to run away from the niggling message that he is truly risen to a new life and is calling us to a new way of living as brothers and sisters of a caring family. Maybe, it is too big a risk. How can we be sure that it is not all an illusion? Today's gospel assures us that if we share our bread with the hungry and shelter the homeless, we will meet and recognise him through the bread we share.

Fourth Sunday of Easter

Jn 10:1-10

To bemoan change and to yearn for the past is to deny the wonder of God's gift of creative adaptability. Structures and institutions must adapt to new needs and opportunities or else become irrelevant quickly. The Church is no exception. The core teaching and values of following Christ remain constant but the most effective way in which they are to be lived out must be discovered and implemented by each generation, learning from the past but living in the present while planning flexibly for the future.

Today is Vocations Sunday. It is an opportunity to focus on how priesthood and religious life will be lived-out in the year 2000 and beyond. However, no matter what happens in the rapidly changing decades of the 21st century, the person called to the priesthood or religious life will be:

One who believes that God is achieving great things in and through this generation;

One who believes that the eucharist is the cornerstone of life;

One whose hope is founded on living faith, shared and nurtured in a praying community;

One who will risk going the extra mile for Christ;

One who will risk surrendering personal freedom for security in the Lord;

One who will risk undertaking the most menial jobs for love of others;

One who will risk being exploited for the sake of the gospel.

Such a one will be a person of hopeful joy rather than of cynical despair; a person of generous risk rather than of comfortable cuteness. Only God's grace could inspire such living. It is open to each of us to create an atmosphere where such a call can take root.

Fifth Sunday of Easter

Jn 14:1-12

The apostle Thomas was very frustrated by the answers Jesus gave him. It is a frustration that could be shared by many hearers of today's gospel. Thomas' request was simple. He wanted straight-forward and clear-cut guidelines on how best to come to God. If the rules were clear and definite, he felt that he could keep them and earn his salvation.

But Jesus did not give him the much-sought-after clarity. Instead, he told him (and us, in turn) that the secret is to gradually get to know Jesus, to live like him and so to grow in a deepening relationship with him. This is the only way to the Father.

Nothing has changed. Some of us at times, and more of us at all times, look for security in human religious regulations, thinking that once these are fulfilled, salvation is guaranteed. Not so, says Jesus. Following him means always being willing to go the extra mile, always to be increasingly generous in prayer and good works, always being willing to let God surprise us with his gifted call to expanding love.

It is in Jesus that we see the fulness of the father's revealed love, the truth about God. He is truly the way, the truth and the life. Listen with the doubting Thomas to the master's message.

Sixth Sunday of Easter

Jn 14:15-21

Contract working rather than permanent employment is becoming a more noticeable feature in our society. The economic climate dictates that the talented and the healthy are paid above the going rate as long as they are highly productive and, after that, even they are discarded.

Investors move their capital to maximise their dividends without regard for the long-serving employees or future job prospects. In sport, the top stars move to the highest bidder with little thought for club or supporters. Loyalty seems to bring little reward and permanence in any relationship is represented as inhibiting full development.

It is an insidiously destructive trend which undermines the unique preciousness of each person. In many spheres, the ethos is to live for today and to shirk the pain involved in the long haul.

Yet, following Christ is a lifelong decision but even heroically generous young folk wonder whether such a long-term commitment is worthwhile or possible. Can happiness and fulfilment be found in dedicating one's whole life to permanent marriage, to loving God and serving others?

True, we fail on occasions to live up to our ideals and many suggest that because of such failures, the vision is unsustainable. But we are loved by a forgiving God who in today's gospel promises us his Spirit who teaches that happiness is reached through keeping his commandments of committed love.

The promise is not only of a teacher but of an advocate, an enabler, one who will live within us as we journey towards the goal.

The Ascension of the Lord

Mt 28:16-20

It is a fact, not a slogan. Our God is one and is a blessed Trinity of three persons in one God. Like many precious things in life, this fact can only be appreciated and not understood. It cannot be discovered but is made known by God through his son Jesus Christ. It is only through faith-filled prayer that we can grow into an awareness of this inner nature of God. To find the exact and apt word to describe another's personality is difficult and usually it is only somebody who is close to the other person who can make an effective attempt at the task. It is only the lover glimpses the unique awesomeness of the loved one. So it is not surprising that before returning to the father, and having promised the Holy Spirit, Jesus sent the apostles out to make disciples of all nations, instructing them to have as the foundation of their work, baptism in the name of the Father, and of the Son and of the Holy Spirit.

This is still the foundation of our faith and the core of Christ's parting message to us.

Seventh Sunday of Easter

Jn 17:1-11

Sunday gospels vary a great deal. Some report on miracles and other noteworthy events in the life of Jesus. Others give aspects of his teaching. But today's gospel is different. It is very special. It is a prayer – the prayer of Jesus before his death, a prayer for his followers, a prayer for you and me.

We need to stop in our busy lives to absorb the extraordinary fact that the Son of God prayed to his Father for each of us, and continues to do so. It is a gospel to be heard in the heart rather than in the head.

He prays that he may give eternal life to everyone who has been entrusted to him. This is his gift to us, to share in the life of God, now and forever. His prayer is that our hearts may be open to receive such a gift and that receiving it we may glorify the one who brought it to us.

To know God is the pinnacle of human life. No other acquisition, achievement or gift can match it. Indeed, all human effort finds its enrichment in so far as it leads to God. Today's gospel is an invitation and an opportunity to absorb something of this wisdom.

Pentecost Sunday

Jn 20:19-23

On every side the pain is obvious. In so many lives, hopelessness and despair are tangible. Hurts, mistakes and failures have diminished all our lives. If only we could start again. If only we could give each other a second chance, another opportunity to live life over again. The 'if only' cry wells up in every human heart sometime and in some hearts all the time, calling out for a reply.

Jesus responds to this anguish in today's gospel. After the savage brutality of Calvary had destroyed an innocent and good friend, the fear-filled disciples had locked themselves away from their enemies and even from their friends. The risen Lord comes among them bringing peace, a spirit of creative love that heals hurt and unravels the web of fear that ensnares wounded human hearts. Strengthened by this enabling power of the Spirit, the disciples are sent out into the world as messengers of forgiveness and hope. Every hurt they forgive is healed through the power of God. Every hope they rekindle is fanned into flame by the Spirit of God. This was the stupendous mystery of the first Pentecost. Jesus renews this miracle each time the people of God gather to meet the risen Lord in the eucharist. He sends the same healing Spirit into our hearts and sends us out to be wounded healers of all whose broken lives touch ours.

Pentecost is a focus time for healing forgiveness, a time to initiate it and to accept it. It is an opportunity not to be missed.

Trinity Sunday

Jn 3: 16-18

A key element in understanding who one is, is to appreciate and accept where one has to come from. Roots are important. To be secure in one's origins is a cornerstone for growing into maturity. To be unwilling to fully accept one's beginnings is a recipe for lifelong frustrations as one searches endlessly for inadequate substitutes.

People identify us by a surname springing from our roots and may often categorise us by our social origins. The people of Jesus' time did it to him. He was son of Joseph, the carpenter from Nazareth and a child of Mary, whose relations were all around the place. Jesus was comfortable and grateful for these roots. Without rejecting them, he gradually grew in a wisdom that enabled him to realise that he was much more, that he was Son of one whom he called Father.

The wonder of this relationship possessed him more and more throughout his life and he strove to share it with the disciples and in turn, with us. This living love relationship between the Father and himself, he called the Spirit whom he promised to send to live in our hearts. Father, Son and Holy Spirit, the awesome core of faith which we celebrate on Trinity Sunday.

Our roots are human but they are more. We come from God and are rooted in God. This is the reason for the hope that is in us, a hope that we must never let any person or circumstance steal from us. To lose such roots would be to be impoverished forever.

Glory be to the Father, the Son and the Holy Spirit.

The Body and Blood of Christ
Jn 6:51-58

Recently, on a truly beautiful evening, I stopped at a roadside church in Kerry to pray evening prayer. The peace and the quiet helped me to enjoy God's presence. Suddenly, the silence was broken by the arrival of a busload of foreign tourists. Cameras clicked and coins jingled in the shrine boxes. After a few minutes, silence returned as the visitors rejoined their bus. There was just one elderly man left standing before the altar. He turned towards me and spoke slowly and solemnly.

'Treasure what you have, Father. For many years now I have lived far from any church or Christian community. It is difficult to keep God's love alive in one's heart on one's own and without the eucharist. Treasure it.'

The horn in the bus hooted angrily and he was gone. I was left to ponder the wonder of God's presence in the eucharist. He is present to us to help us to be present to him. The opportunity to be present to each other in friendship and worship is a gift of a great God.

Today we say thanks for the gift of the Body of Christ, Corpus Christi.

Second Sunday in Ordinary Time

Jn 1:29-34

John the Baptist was to prepare the way for the coming of Jesus. He all but completes the task in today's gospel when he declares that he saw the Spirit coming upon Jesus. This coming of the Spirit shows that Jesus was indeed the promised Messiah and the Baptist says that, through his being a witness to that fundamental fact, he completes the task he was sent to do.

There are similarities and differences between our calling and that of the Baptist. Jesus has come and continues to be present among us through and in the Church. But his presence must become effective daily in each person's life and in the ordinary circumstances of life. How do we prepare for this daily coming?

One crucial way is by sharing our faith and supporting each other in prayer. A temptation of our time is to think that one's salvation is just a matter between God and oneself. It is not. Jesus called us as a people and saved us as a people. Faith and salvation is the business of every follower of Christ. Everybody is called to make his or her contribution to the faith of the community. It starts in the home and overflows into the parish. It is hard to remain faithful to the Lord in today's world but it is all the harder for the lone ranger Christian. The need of our time is to strengthen each other's faith and hope so that the people of God may grow in love. The calling is to bear witness by our shared lives to the fact that we are a people called to praise and thank God as a community and to receive his salvation together.

Third Sunday in Ordinary Time
Mt 4:12-23

It is form-filling time for thousands of students about to leave school. It is a time when they strive to link their ability to their aspirations and to the opportunities available. Even though many options are closed to the majority because of lack of finance or lack of ability, the range of third-level courses on offer is ever-widening.

But no matter how varied the possibilities, the fact remains that each person has only one life. One particular choice rules out another option. This is as true in personal relationships as it is in jobs. One can explore possibilities forever but at the risk of never experiencing the joy and security of commitment to another person, to a job, to a way of life or even to God.

Today's gospel tells of a quartet who made such a commitment in a very radical fashion. Andrew, Peter, James and John left all they had to follow Jesus. It was a choice that led them through glorious moments as well as disappointments to an ever-deepening friendship with Jesus.

God's call to them seems to us to have been very clear-cut, but what was really clear-cut was their response. They did what God asked. Our call is the same.

To have a possibility of happiness one must choose what is really important and set about living out that priority with enthusiasm each day.

Fourth Sunday in Ordinary Time

Mt 5:1-12

Michael has no notions about holiness and certainly he has no ambitions to be canonised. He will settle for a safe pass in the examination to get into heaven. He sees the commandments as the test and so he hopes to get by through avoiding murder, stealing, adultery and through attending Sunday Mass as well as saying a few prayers daily.

The commandments are the basic code by which he lives and judges himself. He will probably view today's gospel as being the honours course and of no great interest to him. That is a big mistake because the guarantee of God's presence in the next life is rooted in recognising his presence in those around us now. The sermon on the mount which we begin in today's gospel is the core of Christ's teaching for his followers. Avoiding evil is only the first step for a disciple of Christ. The next and crucial step is to do good to others and for others in every possible way above and beyond the call of duty. It is to be so generous oneself that being untrammelled by this world's goods, God can give one the kingdom of his friendship. It is to be so merciful to others that there is no hardness of heart blocking one receiving forgiveness oneself. It is to believe that the strength of gentleness rather than the arrogance of power is God's way of building his kingdom. It is to be blessed by God.

With God, there are no pass students. All are honours candidates. Each one of us is called to greatness and is precious in his eyes.

Fifth Sunday in Ordinary Time

Mt 5:13-16

Americans are well known for creating words and catch phrases to describe situations, products or people. They have given us the cookie jar, G.I's and the Five and Ten store. One American has claimed that the Church has become largely a community of gospel-consumers rather than gospel-creators. He uses the phrase gospel-consumers to describe people who avail of all the community and the Church has to offer by way of services, schools, and sacraments but who give little back in return. They admire and may benefit from the community association, the trade union or the Vincent de Paul but they leave it to others to carry the can. They may even enjoy good Sunday liturgy but let others take the trouble of making it happen. They consume what is on offer and then walk away.

Christ has called us to be creators rather than consumers, to serve rather than be served, to be the light of the world by our life-style rather than mere critics of the darkness of the world's selfishness. We live in a polluted atmosphere of get rather than give. The pollution has touched most of us. Today's gospel is a challenge to be a light of unselfishness in the deepening darkness of self-centredness, to be a creator of Christian community rather than just a consumer, to take Christ at his word and to lay down one's life for others.

Sixth Sunday in Ordinary Time
Mt 5:17-37

While I am not a man of no fixed abode, my work takes me into different schools, communities and groups every week. Each one of them is unique and has its own atmosphere and structures. I see more and more clearly now that it is an attitude of hearts rather than a code of rules that makes a school a home from home, a place where pupils and teachers belong, where growth in maturity and love of God can happen. True enough, the rules are important like walls are essential for a house. But walls, no more than rules alone, do not make a home.

In Christ's time, the scribes and pharisees were so hung up on rules that he lost patience with them. Rules should be scaffolding for creating an atmosphere of respect and trust, but they can become mere protectors of self-interest. There is more to good living and virtue than rules. 'If your virtue goes no deeper than the scribes, you will never get into heaven.' Christ challenged the people of his time and he challenges us with: 'You have learnt but I say to you.' He asks for much more than rules from his followers. He asks us to live with growing love in our hearts and to make sure that this love permeates every institution or group to which we belong.

Seventh Sunday in Ordinary Time
Mt 5:38-48

Why be honest? Why avoid drugs? Why be conventional in life-style? Why go to Mass? Why can I not do as I please? Many listening parents and tuned-in teachers are familiar with the endless questioning of teenagers. Whatever about the annoyance at such interminable queries, the fact is that such searching is the road to personal responsibility. Mere conformity to the strongest pressure of the moment leaves the young person very vulnerable in a world of changing pressures. Understanding, appreciation, conviction and owning are the cornerstones of genuine human motivation.

One of the risks of becoming an adult is that we may stop exploring the why of our actions and just settle for what we did before or for what society expects of us. Today's gospel command to forgive anyone who wrongs us raises a question in many hearts. Why should we obey?

The key that enables us to forgive and to do so with joyful enthusiasm come from a deepening grasp of who we are and what we are called to. Each one of us is made by God and is loved unchangingly by him with a love that is unearned and can never be lost. The human temptation is to reject the offender and to love only those who have earned our love. But we are called to imitate God by loving even those who do not deserve such a gift. Forgiveness is the test of such love.

Eighth Sunday in Ordinary Time
Mt 6:24-34

Many years ago, I was told that a preacher should prepare his sermon with the Bible in one hand and the newspaper in the other hand. The idea is that the newspaper reflects and represents the world and life out of which the Bible comes and in which the values and the message of the gospel must be lived. If I were to link them up for today's sermon, there would be immediate conflict. Today's gospel is telling us not to worry about what we are to eat or what we are to wear. On the other hand, the newspapers continue to bring news of job losses and the lack of prospects for the young, not to mention new taxes. It seems unrealistic to tell a family whose breadwinner is out of work and whose teenage children may never get jobs, not to worry. So how is this gospel story meaningful in our time?

Frankly, I am not sure. I see that for those of us who are reasonably secure and have enough on the table, it is challenging us not to set our hearts on material goods and not to put our total trust in them. There are more important matters.

But for those who are without food, shelter or other necessities of life, what is the message for them? Maybe it is telling them not to worry because the Father knows their needs and he trusts their more well-off brothers and sisters in Christ to care for those needs of money, work, security and respect. Is that trust by the Father misplaced? That is the question we answer by how we live.

Ninth Sunday in Ordinary Time
Mt 7:21-27

It was overcast but dry when we left the car at the entrance to the mountain forest. It was a good day to explore new territory. The trails through the forest were well maintained and we made rapid progress up the hillside. Unexpectedly, mist and rain whirled around us and we were forced to turn back in haste. We came to a fork in the trail. Which one was the way back to the car? A sign-post would have been a welcome blessing but, of course, there was none. My instinct told me to take the left hand one. As it turned out, my instinct was wrong. My mistake sent us miles off route and we were cold, tired, hungry and miserable when eventually, we reached the car late in the day.

Life is often like a mountain trail with forks or junctions along the way. We choose a blessing or a curse, to do good or evil, to create or to destroy, to enrich or to impoverish, to build love or hate. Our instinct sometimes tells us that selfishness and pleasure is the route to take. That instinct can be wrong. God's teaching is the signpost to a better route, a surer way to human happiness. We ignore it at our peril. Otherwise, it might be very late in life that we find our true way home.

This is the warning of today's gospel.

Tenth Sunday

Mt 9:9-13

Exclusivity through wealth, social class, gender, race or religion has long been a feature of human living. Excluding people because of their gender or the colour of their skin, leads to an outcry in our time. Such exclusion is obviously unjust. Using merit or achievement as standards of admission seems more reasonable at first sight but even these criteria are open to question too. Certainly the decision of Jesus to admit sinners to his kingdom and to exclude the just seems grossly unfair to those who have kept the rules and tried to live their lives by God's laws as they saw them. Maybe Jesus could be arraigned under equal opportunity legislation! But this could only happen if somebody was found to initiate the case, a just one free from sin, one who did not need God's forgiveness. Jesus is forcefully pointing out that everyone needs God's gift of salvation, given to all open to receive it. Indeed the lesson is that God's greatest welcome is for those who have least, who need him most and who know their need. Such is the core of God's plan. His way is not our way and we often operate in exactly the opposite way. We are most happy to welcome into our lives and homes those who need us least but who can benefit us most. So when the opportunity offers, we welcome the influential, the well off, the established achievers rather than the failures – the homeless, the sick, those who cannot cope with life. One big risk in such behaviour is that it blinds us to the wonder of how God treats us and so destroys our inner peace. This gospel is a challenge to be converted in our life-style so that we may be open to receive the gift of God's unconditional love for us.

Eleventh Sunday

Mt 9:36 – 10:8

Today's gospel is a dangerous one. The danger lies in the proba-
bility of its being heard merely as the call of the twelve apostles,
with its challenges directed to them and to their successors, the
clerics in the Church today. The call is more profound and widespread and is directed to each one of us.

Jesus was and is moved by the plight of the harassed, the poor, the
deprived, the leaderless in society, the sheep without a shepherd.
Their needs are many. The task is enormous. The opportunity for
harvest is great but so few are willing to spend themselves at it.

So, today's gospel is about recruiting workers who will care for
God's people, who will build his kingdom of justice and love.
Each one can make even a little contribution to the ethos of service
rather than to the atmosphere of selfishness each day. It may be
only a drop in the ocean but without raindrops there would be no
ocean. True enough, to achieve a fairer world would need new
economic structures, but in the meantime, each one can lighten
another's load and strengthen another's faith.

Twelfth Sunday

Mt 10:26-33

The house is very quiet as I write. The part of the college where I live with over a hundred young men preparing for priesthood is deserted apart from myself. Most have left on holidays. The others are gone to be ordained priests among their own people. To go forward for ordination nowadays, they must have great courage in their hearts, courage to do what they know is right for them, to do always what God wants for the rest of their lives.

They go out to serve in a world that puts more value on wealth than on faith in God, that rates achievement higher than integrity, that responds to power pressure rather than to peoples' needs, that seeks happiness in individual comfort rather than in relationship, and that ignores loneliness under the guise of preserving privacy.

The young priest's call is to create communities where Christ's values replace the world's priorities. It is a call to courage, to stand up for what is right no matter what the cost, to prefer God to all else.

But, of course, this is the call of every Christian – priest, religious or lay, each in their own way of life. Every Christian's role is to make Christ's presence tangible in the family, in the neighbourhood, in the work-place and among those in greatest need. To do this requires great courage, the courage not to be afraid of those who can destroy one's livelihood. As Christ puts it in today's gospel: 'Do not be afraid of those who kill the body but cannot kill the soul.'

Thirteenth Sunday

Mt 10:37-42

'Comfort brings contentment' is one of the greatest heresies of our time. A core ingredient of current advertising is to persuade one and all that the highest point of human achievement is personal comfort. This pervasive illusion woos each of us constantly and undermines genuine human happiness.

To live in the belief that we are created only to be bemused by possessions, bewitched by television, befuddled by alcohol, is to lose sight of the greatness of the Christian human calling. This calling is to love another and to be outward bound rather than self-seeking, while keeping alive faith and hope in each other and in God.

It is a calling that emphasises giving rather than grasping, serving rather than being served, forgiving rather than retaliating, rejoicing in another's good fortune rather than belittling the goodness of others. It is a life that demands a willingness to sacrifice one's selfishness every day.

Jesus puts it strongly in today's gospel when he reminds us that it is only those who are willing to take up this daily cross who can be his disciples. There is no room for compromise. The way he offers is the way he travelled himself before us. It is the way to lasting joy.

Fourteenth Sunday
Mt 11:25-30

Five-year-old Kevin was busy at the kitchen table with his markers drawing God. Seven-year-old Ciara with all the theological wisdom of First Communion behind her, asserted that nobody knows what God is like. Kevin claimed that they would when he was finished drawing him.

The confidence of the young is disarming. But, seriously, how well does each of us know our God? What qualities of God are uppermost in our prayers and in our hearts? What words do we use to describe him?

Today's gospel is very specific. It highlights the gentleness of God. 'Learn from me for I am gentle and humble of heart and you will find rest for your soul.' So the message is to grow in appreciation of God's gentleness towards us so that, in turn, we may be gentle towards ourselves and towards others.

Gentleness is born out of appreciation of who and what we are. God sees us as his own, redeemed by his only Son, precious to his eyes, vulnerable, and so he treats us with a kindness that knows no bounds. This is both reassuring and challenging. The reassurance is that God will always treat us with a tenderness that the wounded need and relish. The challenge is for us to do the same both to ourselves and to everyone else in our lives without exception. It is the ruling out of exceptions that presents the real challenge.

Fifteenth Sunday
Mt 13:1-23

Seed sowing is a task for those with hope for the future in their hearts. Not realising that hoarded seed will eventually decompose, the faint-hearted never have the nerve to sow in the expectation of a crop in due time. No hoarder can be a disciple of Jesus. He expects each of his followers to be sowers of goodness and of gospel everywhere.

Some of the scattered seed will fall on rocky ground bearing little or no fruit, but much of it will bear fruit 30, 60 or 100 fold as today's gospel assures us. We cannot always judge or choose the human soil, but our vocation is to be extravagant in scattering goodness around us, sharing our time, talent, care, energy and our faith.

For the followers of Jesus, sowing the seeds of faith and tending the seedlings of gospel living among the young is always a privileged task, no matter how onerous or futile it seems to be. Sowing is our business. The harvest is the Lord's responsibility.

Sixteenth Sunday

Mt 13:24-43

The flow of traffic was unusually heavy for the late evening. Stopped next to me on the footpath was an athlete in full gear. Already he is in training for next year's marathon. He never misses a training session as he believes that there is no such thing as instant strength. It only grows gradually as do courage, fidelity, generosity, love and faith.

Within each of us, we find that goodness only grows very slowly. In fact, side by side with our better selves, weakness and evil continue to survive within us. In their anxiety to lead us to a better way of living, preachers sometimes forget that instant conversions are very rare and so they challenge us to root out all evil once and for all. Not so, Christ. In today's gospel he gives a message of hope and stresses the need for patience and endurance. Even though, despite our best efforts, we find the darnel of sin and selfishness still in our lives, the main crop of goodness will bring a harvest of reward. With so much injustice and failure around us and within us, the temptation is to despair of achieving anything worthwhile. Christ's message is that the seedlings of goodness may have to grow in the midst of the weeds of selfishness, but his seed sown in our hearts will eventually yield a great harvest. We must not lose heart but nurture every glimmer of goodness wherever we find it. Today's Mass strengthens us for the task.

Seventeenth Sunday

Mt 13:44-52

Change in the Church has been a feature of our lifetime. For some the change has been too much, for others not enough. For some it is too radical, for others too superficial. For many the change has been from certainty to search, from clearly laid down guidelines to taking the responsibility of applying the gospel to one's daily life oneself. No matter how desirable, this change from conformity to conviction is not an easy one. The danger is that instead of conviction we settle for compromise. Obviously compromise is essential in many areas of life. People with different perspectives must respect the unique preciousness of each other and the right of the other to hold positions at variance with one's own. But compromise has a destructive as well as a constructive side.

Compromise with truth leads to mistrust and disharmony. Compromise with honesty leads to greed and violence, with fidelity leads to shattered promises and separated families, with temperance leads to drunkenness and personal disintegration. Some things are so precious that we must protect them even at great cost. Compromise in our own individual hearts with what is important to us is like a creeping weed that overuns everything unless it receives frequent attention.

The temptation in our time is to live as if we can hold on to a comfortable self-centred way of life and have the Spirit of Jesus as well. In today's gospel, the finder gave all he had to acquire a pearl of great price. We have a similar opportunity each day as we choose to dally with compromise or to live so that gradually we grow into a conviction that God loves us and that we should live accordingly.

Eighteenth Sunday

Mt 14:13-21

I love a stroll through the city streets on the long summer evenings. It was there I met Jimmy. He was scavenging for food in the refuse bags awaiting collection. We sat and talked. He had good luck in his search that evening. He was happy about that but could not understand why people are so wasteful about God's gifts. He pointed to extravagance and waste in all aspects of how we live, not just what we deliberately waste but what we use or eat without really needing it. He reminded me that most of the world went to bed hungry. He was a good preacher as he sent me home thoughtful.

Then I read today's gospel and two things struck home immediately. Firstly, there was Christ's command to the disciples that they themselves should give the hungry something to eat. Secondly, we read that after the miracle of the loaves and fishes, they gathered up the leftovers in case they would be wasted.

Jimmy's wisdom, Christ's command and the gatherers' diligence left me pondering on my own way of life.

Nineteenth Sunday
Mt 14:22-33

To be human is to be a risk-taker. Every choice we make involves risk. Even the food we eat involves some risk. But, of course, it also nourishes our body. Like every risk, there are two sides to it and maturity consists in being able to assess the risk accurately.

Some risks are more obvious than others.When Jesus called Peter to come to him across the water, the most obvious risk was one of drowning. Yet, there was an opportunity to meet the master, to trust him, to show one's faith in him. Peter's choice was stark, to risk drowning or to refuse the call of Jesus. Sunday's gospel tells us the choice Peter made.

Similar choices face us in following Christ. For some there is the risk of giving up the security of job or career to follow him in full-time ministry. There is the risk that it will not work out. For others, there is the risk involved in committing oneself to another in permanent Christian marriage. It, too, may not work out as planned. For the single person, the risk is in living a life of outgoing generous love and service where the care may not be reciprocated.

In these choices, the possible loss involved is sometimes much more obvious than the gain. It takes the wisdom of the spirit of God to discern and decide which risks are worth taking. Some can never take the risk of trusting themselves or God. This inability is a serious handicap because the road to happiness consists in choosing the truly best option and in following it through. Peter did that and walked on water with the help of Jesus.

Twentieth Sunday

Mt 15: 21-28

Hungry people appreciate food with a relish unknown to the regularly well-fed. Indeed, the well-fed are often finicky about what they eat and critical about what is on offer, feeling that they deserve better. The Canaanite woman in today's gospel had no illusions of such privilege. She knew her need. Her daughter was ill and needed the touch of the master's healing power. Better than any of the religious people in the crowd, she knew what she needed and was prepared to pester the master until she got it.

Her persistence has a lesson for us all. We can be distracted by a surfeit of activity, comfort, work, success, sport or even, of religion. En route, we lose that urgent and keen awareness of our need. We rarely look for spiritual sustenance. Our faith, hope and love can die of starvation. We rarely pester God to deepen our awareness of his love for us. If only we were as aware as the Canaanite woman of what God could do for us, what a difference it would make in our lives.

Twenty-First Sunday
Mt 16:13-20

I sat quietly on the lakeshore watching the artist sketch and colour. Gradually, the grandeur of mountain and lake, forest and undergrowth, sunshine and shadow were caught in his emerging picture. It was a privileged moment to be an onlooker at such a creation. Undoubtedly, this artist had many gifts – an eye for colour, an appreciation of nature's harmony and an understanding of perspective. But he was a dedicated craftsman as well. Conscious of his gifts, he had studied the texture of his materials, the blending of colours and a myriad of other aspects of his creative work. He had made art a priority in life. Gift and response were combined within him with great results on canvas.

Such a combination will always bear great fruit especially in our relationship with God. Faith is a gift, as Peter is reminded in today's gospel. It was not his own intelligence alone that enabled him to recognise Jesus as Son of God but the revelation that had been given him by the Father. God's gift of knowledge of himself is crucial but so too is our response. Gifts can be ignored or they can be appreciated, explored and enjoyed. Faith is accepted and developed by giving prime time to prayer. There is no other way. The crunch in faith development is making God a priority in our lives.

Just as the artist's gift could remain dormant and even die, so too could our faith. Today's gospel call is to ask for the gift and then to nurture it daily.

Twenty-Second Sunday
Mt 16:21-27

We live in the age of a great lie. It is subtle, all pervasive and generally accepted by most of us most of the time but it is still untrue. It is the assumption, the attitude, that all pain and discomfort should be instantly curable, that only the comfortably easy is worth seeking, that every whim should be explorable without the cost, that self-denial restricts human development, that self-fulfilment is the only goal, that we can and should live in a perfect world. We do not live in such a world nor was it God's plan that we should. His vision is much broader. It allows us to live in a world where we can grow and develop in faith, hope and love through adversity and difficulty, as well as through giftedness and blessing, as caring brothers and sisters. The temptation of our time is to accept every benefit that comes our way as if it were our right while closing our hearts to the needs of our contemporaries and of those who will come after us.

The danger of being seduced by such a treacherous illusion is so great that Jesus warns us in toay's gospel to offset such restricting self-centredness. He challenges us to see opportunities for developing love by sacrificing ourselves for others, by taking up our daily cross, by making room in our lives for God and for his plans for our happiness. We ignore to our great loss the fact that sometimes love is tested and even enriched through shared suffering and that success, comfort and ease can endanger love more easily than pain and sacrifice. It is an arresting gospel message.

Twenty-Third Sunday
Mt 18:15-20

It seemed like a caring and innocuous remark, but it sparked off an inferno. David had a few drinks. Jack who liked a drink himself, but who was on the dry for Sunday's match, suggested that he would drive home. David blew up. He saw Jack's suggestion as a reprimand and accused him of self-righteousness. David drove off angrily and erratically. Jack walked home chastened.

It was just the type of situation that today's gospel does not seem to visualise, when it suggests that each of us has an obligation to point out faults to another, in love, of course, and with a view to enabling the errant one to reform. This gospel counsel seems somewhat idealistic and very risky but also challenging. True enough, it is a great act of friendship to point out to another the error of his or her ways, and to be able to do it so that the other person responds constructively is a great gift, and a blessing beyond compare for the friendship. But it is a delicate task calling for great sensitivity and wisdom on both sides.

Today's gospel is an opportunity to pray for such sensitive wisdom in all our relationships so that all may be done in Christ's name.

Twenty-Fourth Sunday
Mt 18:21-35

Forgiveness is a many-sided feature of interpersonal relation-ships. Many find it hard to forgive, but more find it hard to accept forgiveness fully in a way that nurtures deepening harmony. The crux about fruitfully accepting forgiveness is that one must firstly admit to oneself and to another that one has failed, while holding firmly to the belief that one is still precious and loveable no matter what the failure.

Combining such honesty and self-esteem is not always easy. It does not come naturally but has to be learned through practice and supportive experience. Our first instinct is to be self-defensive. We seek to excuse our failure and to emphasise our independence rather than our interdependence. Maturity brings us to realise that we are not lone rangers but a pilgrim people who share a wonder-ful but limited human nature on the journey to glory. Limitation implies probable failure. Failure will always need forgiveness.

A key element in the Christian calling is to enable one another to accept forgiveness and thus be open to the growth in love which God wishes to work in us. This enabling demands that we forgive each other respectfully and generously in little things every day so that we grow in an attitude of open-heartedness and trust.

Twenty-Fifth Sunday
Mt 20:1-16

Serious strikes scarred the work-place recently. Fear and selfishness seem to have been key factors in these heart-breaking situations. The risk of loss of jobs, of bonuses, of promotional opportunities evoked the defensive fear response in many hearts. Selfishness is often related to fear as people grasp for more lest they miss out on something another gets. Selfish fear is a powerful force in our human make-up but is an unreliable foundation for building true harmony and community.

Today's gospel has an important point to make as a balance to this dangerous emotion. It is the gospel story of the workers who received the same wages even though some worked much shorter hours. It looks like a charter for chaos in industrial relations. But to read it that way is to miss the point that Jesus is making. He is reminding us that every talent, brain or skill is a gift of God and does not entitle us to a more privileged position than those less gifted than ourselves.

This gospel is a stern reminder that we owe all we are to God so we need to constantly curb our selfishness. It is also a reassurance that God does not reward our achievements but our responses to the opportunities that come our way. The message is a brake on our selfishness and an antidote to our fears.

Twenty-Sixth Sunday
Mt 21:28-32

Lip service is a common disease. It afflicts most of us even if only subconsciously, a lot of the time. We say that each person is uniquely precious, but so often we value the talented and successful more highly that those who do not quite make it. We express sympathy for the homeless, but resent when housing them would interfere with our own life-styles or pockets.

A common phenomenon is to speak approvingly of equality, fair play, respect, truth, family life but to shy away from the sacrifice and commitment actually involved in protecting these values. We do not let ourselves hear the cry of the poor, of the powerless, of the wronged, of the deprived, of God himself. We shelter behind custom, accepted practice or institutionalised privilege.

Things were little different in the time of Jesus as we hear in today's gospel. He lost patience with the establishment of his time who learnedly quibbled about his teaching and then ignored it, whereas the rejects of society were open to conversion.

Conversion means admitting that one has not lived up to God's call but that now one is prepared to try again to do so. Such sincerity far out-weighs weakness. It is not failure that Jesus condemns but the hypocrisy of saying the generous thing and doing the opposite – and feeling self-righteous in the process.

The kingdom of heaven is for those who are prepared to answer God's call today, no matter what happened yesterday.

Twenty-Seventh Sunday
Mt 21:33-43

Absentee landlords have had a bad history in rural Ireland, especially in the last century. For the most part, they extracted every last penny from their defenceless tenants. As a class, they were resented, hated and even cursed. Consequently, to find Jesus in today's gospel using the image of an absentee landlord to teach us may not be the most congenial image for those with long familial memories. Whatever about the suitability of the image in the Irish scene, the message is crystal clear.

The father has given us certain abilities, aptitudes, skills and opportunities and he expects us to produce a return of worship and prayer towards himself and of generous care towards our fellow human beings. Rather than do just that, the privileged ones in the gospel story, the tenants, executed the son and heir.

We do something similar when we deny in practice that all God's gifts are given for all people. We do that by usurping more than we really need to live. The tenor of our times is one of self-centred, material comfort and security.

Christ's call is to be satisfied with less, so leaving more for those in need. Today's invitation is to recognise again God's ownership of everything on this earth and so to experience the joy of sharing which far surpasses the frustration of grabbing.

Twenty-Eighth Sunday
Mt 22:1-14

As well as gratitude and admiration, great generosity often evokes suspicion in some hearts. Unsolicited generosity, especially, sometimes causes people to question the motivation of the big hearted donor. The first reaction is to query what does the giver receive in return. We find it hard to believe that there may be no return. The human condition makes us sceptical about disinterested unselfishness in anybody. As a result we may even doubt God's generosity.

So Jesus goes to great trouble to convince us of God's unconditional self-giving. One of the central parables he uses is today's story of all and sundry being invited to the wedding feast. The feast is a symbol of God's sharing himself with us. Some reject the invitation to be part of God's people and so lose out on eternal life. Others accept the invitation at first but then refuse to live as God asks and their loss is just as great. It is not that God withdraws the gift but that their selfish life-style prevents them from accepting it.

The question is not why does God love so recklessly but why do we not let such love melt our hearts so that we would live forever dressed in the wedding garment of his friendship?

Twenty-Ninth Sunday
Mt 22:15-21

It happens in many areas of life. The motorist trapped in a traffic jam denounces the failure of the traffic wardens to prosecute those illegal parkers who hinder the traffic flow. Of course, when it is convenient for the same disgruntled one to park inconsiderately, the intervention of a traffic warden is labelled harassment. Vocal parents can advocate that strict discipline be enforced in school but when one of their own children is suspended, the head teacher is considered inflexible and lacking in understanding of modern youth. In other words, we accept and use social institutions when it suits and we decry them or ignore them when there is some cost involved.

Something similar was prevalent in the time of Jesus. Many religious Jews found it convenient to use the Roman currency for daily living and that was acceptable. But all Jews resented paying taxes to the occupying power. This resentment seemed a good snare to trap Jesus but the accompanying inconsistency provided an escape route. If he supported the tax, he lost face with the Jews. If he denounced it, the Romans would eliminate him. His clever side-step of 'Render to Caesar the things that are Caesar's and to God, the things that are God's' challenges us to examine our own inconsistent approaches. We look to teachers to form our young to the highest standards but we ignore the times when our lifestyle of petty lies or alcohol abuse undermines school's good work. More insidiously, we blame God when things go wrong and ignore him when life runs smoothly. If we are to render to God the things that are God's, prayer of thanksgiving as well as of intercession must be part of everyday living. One cannot employ God as a casual cure all. He offers and asks for more constant commitment.

Thirtieth Sunday

Mt 22:34-40

Love is always inventive. No matter what the obstacles, it always finds a way to express itself. Novels, plays and films strive to surpass each other in showing dramatically how courage, generosity, tenderness, ingenuity and endurance comes into play as the lover seeks the loved one. Genuine love enables the lover to break out of the shell of fearfilled self-centredness that always surrounds the one who does not love.

Today's gospel reminds us that we are called to and capable of such inventive love of one another without exception. It is not that we are simply asked to help the neighbour in need when there is no easy escape or nobody else around to do it. The commandment is much more creative and rewarding. It is an invitation to explore, to seek out, to be sensitive to the myriad of ways in which we can respond to another in love by respect, by presence, by word, as well as by sharing and caring.

Expressed love blossoms. The gospel message is to love the neighbour as oneself with a constructive spirit that evokes bonding between the lover and the loved one. This foundation commandment is about living joy rather than about mere duty. To allow oneself to experience it is a blessing from God.

Thirty-First Sunday
Mt 23:1-12

Each generation is quick to spot and articulate the limitations and weaknesses of other generations. The young may see the elders as bossy, too safe, intimidated by what the neighbours think, living in yesterday's world, not living out their professed values and beliefs. The oldies, in return, often feel that the young today have lost respect for their elders, do not appreciate their opportunities, are losing the faith, will only do what suits them and are unwilling to commit themselves long-term.

True enough, each generation sees many good things in the other as well, but the less desirable traits often get more than their share of attention. The reason for this imbalance is fear. We discover that we do not measure up to the ideals that we ourselves or others set for us and to shield ourselves from the pain of our inadequacies we focus on the failures of others to compensate for our own weakness.

A particular focus for our critical eye are those whose role it is to lead, to keep a vision of God's kingdom alive today, to proclaim his goodness and his commandments. So often, such people fail themselves to practise what they preach. The failure weakens the impact of the message, and often we have to live the gospel call without the help of consistent and persuasive example.

Such is the human condition which we share. But the human failure does not invalidate the truth or the power of the gospel. To shelter behind weakness, our own or another's, to avoid God's call to accept his love and to love, is to build one's happiness on shifting sands. God has given us better foundations.

Thirty-Second Sunday

Mt 25:1-13

'We were not married properly at all,' is a common comment from the older generation when they see the fuller participation of the bride and groom in today's religious ceremony. Of course, the genuine marriage still calls for the same commitment and sacrifices as it always did, and in turn, it nurtures security, love and joy in the committed. The core remains the same, the ceremony has changed. In our time the words of self-giving and acceptance together with the exchange of rings are seen as the focal point. In Christ's time, the groom went to the bride's house to claim her and the procession back to his house was regarded as the centrepiece of the marriage ceremony. This usually happened in the late evening, so the procession with the bridesmaids was a torchlight one. In those days it was the bridegrooms who were notoriously bad timekeepers, so there could be a long vigil at the bride's house. No one knew exactly when he would come.

Christ's hearers were only too familiar with that situation and so, in today's gospel, he uses it to highlight the need to be always ready for God's call. While his final call in death seems crucial, we must be always vigilant for his daily calls to love and serve him so that we will be ready to go to him and with him.

Thirty-Third Sunday

Mt 25:14-30

Going for gold is increasingly dominant in the motivation of many young people. Inculcated from an early age, the popular viewpoint is that to achieve happiness one must be better than others. One must win first place to be successful. Even the silver and bronze are regarded as poor substitutes for the gold medal of the outright winner.

The destructive results of such an attitude often remain hidden but always surface eventually. Indeed, the incentive created by this drive to best one's peers does encourage people to develop talents and potential that might otherwise lie dormant. But while such development can be worthwhile, the cost is that it obscures the unique preciousness of each individual. It undermines faith in God's plan for us as a pilgrim people travelling the road of life together, rejoicing in one another's gifts as they are revealed without need to upstage anybody. In brief, it destroys the foundation of lasting inner peace.

Today's gospel tells of the person of few gifts who was so intimidated by the multi-talented that he was unable or unwilling to make the most of the gifts he had. Such intimidation is still rampant. Many ordinary people are slow to realise that their contribution can really affect the quality of life around us. But when the 'little' people of our society accept their giftedness, truly great things are achieved. Today is a call to explore our gifts for loving service and to make the most of them always. To be successfully happy, one does not have to be better than anybody, rather one has to be just one's own best.

Our Lord Jesus Christ, Universal King

(Thirty-fourth Sunday of Ordinary Time)

Mt 25:31-46

The story of a life is sometimes found in a pair of hands. An old man's hands, gnarled like an oak tree, tell of years of toil on the motorways, tunnels and building sites of Britain. The soft lily-white hands of another tell of an affluence that allowed for care and protection all through the years. Some hands are hardened with grit almost ingrained into them. Others are ravaged by the demands of life. Each pair of hands has a history and it is on that history, each one will be judged at the final call. As today's gospel puts it on the feast of Christ the King: 'I was hungry and you gave me to eat; naked and you clothed me. I was in prison and you visited me.'

Our hands may be clenched in unforgiving aggression or may reach out in friendship. They may grasp at everything within reach or may open in a sharing of God's gifts. The letter they write may be a message of hate or it may be a note of goodwill.

Which will my hands do in the days ahead? It is on that answer I will be judged.

St Patrick's Day

Lk 10:1-12, 17-20

Over the last few weeks, millions of Patrick's Day cards have circled the earth. Old bonds have been nurtured. Spirits have been lifted through being remembered. Patrick's Day evokes a feeling of belonging in many hearts. For some, the belonging is to an emigrant race spread throughout the world. For others, it is being part of a beleaguered people fighting for freedom or culture. For a minority, the attraction is jovial ties celebrated through alcohol. For the majority, the bond surely is a lived faith and heritage, preserved through persecution and shared with the world through emigration and mission.

What would St Patrick himself think of it all? As he surveys the scene, there is much that he would be proud of from the giant St Patrick's Cathedrals to the many Fathers Patrick leading eucharistic communities throughout the world. At home and abroad, the gospel-inspired generosity of the Irish still feeds many a hungry mouth, nurses many a weary invalid and brings Christ to many a yearning heart. The seed Patrick sowed still bears much fruit. But if saints can have doubts, perhaps, he would wonder whether the Irish who kept the gospel alive through generations of persecution, will now allow it to be surreptitiously stolen from them through creeping materialism in this one generation. It could happen and it will take more than green shamrocks and golden harps to prevent such a calamity. It will take men and women of faith, courage, generosity and love who can hear and heed Christ's call in the midst of so many pagan attractions, as Patrick did. It is they who must create in our midst communities where the gospel is seen to be lived and not just preached.

The Assumption of the Blessed Virgin Mary

Lk 1:39-56

Today is Show Day in some places. Other venues have regattas. For some industrial workers, today is the last day of the holidays. Many people regard the summer as being over once the 15th of August has come. For Christ, today is his Mother's Day. Parents often have the joy of seeing their children well established in life with their own homes and families. Such parents enjoy sharing in all the success of their offspring especially if they have been through tough times with them.

There is no doubt that Christ and his mother, Mary, were through tough times together. Mary was on Calvary to see her one and only executed as a criminal. The resurrection followed and Christ returned to his father. It seems only natural that, when his Mother came to die, Christ should take her to his own home in heaven. This is the event we remember and celebrate today on the feast of the Assumption of Mary, Mother of God.

Mission Sunday

Mt 9:35-37

Some weeks ago, the rowan trees attracted my attention with their plentiful crop of red berries. I had never seen them so laden either in city parks or in their natural mountain homes. Now from Armagh to Waterford, it is the heavily laden apple trees that catch the eye. I am told that the abundance is largely due to the suitability of the weather for pollination during the month of May. At that time, almost unnoticed, the bees were busily engaged bringing pollen from one flower to its neighbour. The work of months ago is literally bearing plentiful fruit today.

Something similar has happened in the Church. In many Third World countries like Nigeria or the Philippines, there are thriving Christian communities who are making the gospel of Christ a living reality for their people. These vibrant young Churches are the fruit of decades of almost hidden missionary work. Like diligent and industrious bees, the missionaries brought the life-giving pollen of the gospel to blend with and to fructify the religious sense of those to whom they were sent. This is the task that must be undertaken again and again in each generation. Today's world at home and abroad needs the message of Christ's gospel as never before.

Today is Mission Sunday which focuses our attention on the success and the urgency of the whole Church's missionary effort. It is an achievement of which the Irish people can be justifiably proud. It is an undertaking that must evoke so generous a response that our giving demands sacrifice.

May the Lord reward you. He surely will.

All Saints

Mt 5:1-12

While most believers would hope to be saints sometime, some fantasise about being great sinners for a little while beforehand, to taste the 'good life,' to sample pleasure untrammelled by fidelity, to indulge in selfishness without the strictures of justice, to seek revenge without concern for peace. Like many lesser ones, such a fantasy can never be realised. Just as one cannot draw a square circle, one cannot give priority to Christ's values and the world's values at the same time. One has to choose.

Today's Feast of All Saints is the victory celebration of those who chose Christ's way. The gospel outlines the contrast starkly. The mighty are humbled, the hungry are fed and truly blessed are those who seek God with an undivided heart.

The option of the beatitudes has to be made again and again throughout life. Progress may be slow but the important thing is to be on the right road by choosing Christ's way at each fork and by retracing our steps when we do not choose him. Such choices lead us home to be at peace with God and with all the saints.

The Immaculate Conception
Lk 1:26-38

Technology is changing the face of industry. The microchip puts workers on a three day week. Science continues to reveal the secrets of nature in ever new and fascinating ways. Deepening faith leads Christians to explore the mysteries of our God.

A mystery is just not something that we cannot understand. It is reality that we can appreciate more deeply forever and never fully master. Mystery is not a barrier to understanding but an invitation to appreciation.

God's plan to become man through the co-operation of a young village girl is mystery in its deepest sense. The wonder of the Creator entrusting his incarnation to Mary is awesome. How extraordinary that relationship and love between them must have been. It is not surprising that he specially prepared her for the suffering and the glory.

We stand in awe of that mystery today.

Year B

First Sunday in Advent

Mk 13:33-37

The ability to recognise and to take one's chances in life is an essential ingredient for success in business, in sport, in politics and, indeed, in love. Some are slow to follow up on the opportunities of the moment and spend their lives bemoaning the might-have-beens of the past. Others see the chance to sell well, to buy cutely, to put themselves forward persuasively, to jump on the bandwagon towards their chosen goal. Seeing the chance, they take it.

This is what Advent is about and it starts this weekend. It is a timely reminder to take stock and to see what exactly is on offer in this one life each of us has. It is an invitation to see where the popular current of life is taking us and deciding whether this is where we wish to be when the final call comes. Reminding us that we so often repeat the mistakes of previous generations as well as our own, Isaiah warns us against blaming God for the opportunities we let slip. While Paul encourages us to give thanks for the many gifts we have received through Jesus Christ, Mark's gospel admonition is to be alert to the opportunity for good which is on offer now. It will not come again.

Be on your guard, stay awake, because you never know when the time will come.

Second Sunday in Advent

Mk 1:1-8

It was a wet cold December Friday. It had been a particularly busy week for me and I was under pressure to write my reflection in time for the next day's *Examiner*. The attempt was not going too well. The ring on the doorbell was very insistent. I answered with bad grace. My friend Joe needed help. In fact, he needed a pair of shoes badly. I had three pairs. He would be grateful for one. An earlier illness had left him unable to put on his shoes. I knelt to take off his tattered worn ones. As I struggled with the soggy worn laces, the gospel lines came alive and burned within me. The lines were those of John the Baptist that after himself would come the Christ, the strap of whose sandal he was not worthy to untie. For me that day, Christ was living in my friend in need. Christ has assured us that what we do for each other, we do for him. Truly, I was privileged to care for Joe.

Today's gospel has those same lines of John the Baptist. Along with Joe's friendship, they will remain etched forever in my heart.

Third Sunday in Advent

Jn 1:6-8, 19-28

Newspapers devote a great deal of space to court cases. This is a sure sign of public interest. Much of the interest is awakened by the conflict of evidence that frequently arises. Often the judge's or the jury's verdict is based on the integrity of a witness. The judge decides that one witness must be believed rather than the other. Such a decision is sometimes influenced by a person who vouches for the truthfulness of the key witness. Obviously the life-style and character of the one who vouches for another, must itself be well known and above reproach.

Today's gospel tells of one such person, John the Baptist. He was well known to the scribes and pharisees and to other traditional Jews of his time. They could not but admire his simple life-style. He obviously courted nobody's favour. He spoke the truth, especially the need to be reconciled to God while there was still time. His message and his life were so persuasive that some questioned whether he was the promised messenger from God, the Messiah. His reply was sharp. He was only a witness. One much greater than he was to come among them. John came to vouch for the fact that Jesus was the promised one. Some believed him because of the authentic witness of his life.

Our call is to be witnesses to the same Jesus. Will our preparation for Christmas be authentic enough to convince anybody, but especially the young, that the core of Christmas for us is the celebration of the love of God which the birth of Jesus brings us? Our responsibilities and opportunities are enormous. We must not shirk them.

Fourth Sunday of Advent

Lk 1:26-38

A mother's experience of birth is special to her. It is an experience that the rest of us can only glimpse at. True enough, the birth of his child can be awesome and anxiously exciting for the father but his experience is different. The mother's role is one of ever present commitment with all its hopes and expectations, its fears and anxieties, its pain and joy. So much to be thought of in advance, provision to be made for today and for tomorrow, the need to be ready in the midst of routine living, ready for the expected one who may arrive unexpectedly.

All of this must have been heightened for Mary as she journeyed homeless to Bethlehem, unsure of what the day would bring. But she had committed herself at the Annunciation to bring Jesus into the world. She was the handmaid of the Lord and the birth of Jesus was a peak moment in her response to the call.

Today's gospel takes us back to the Annunciation as it is Mary and all mothers who teach us to focus on the birth in the midst of the many things that have to be done at this festive time. A mother will always be aware of the central reality, so being with Mary this week will keep alive our faith in the mystery of God's coming among us. As well as being Mary's day, we could make today our mother's day in the run up to Christmas.

Christmas

Lk 2:1-14

The man at the door needed the price of a night's lodging. It gradually transpired that he needed a little more. He had a wife and child. They were homeless and hungry. The temptation to investigate the reason for his sorry plight was strong. If he were genuinely deserving, one could help but one would not want to be had. There are so many characters around nowadays. However, cross-examination can be so disrespectful especially to those to whom life has dealt a weaker hand. It is good to be interested and caring but so hard to keep prejudice at bay. The comfortably successful are always prejudiced against the impoverished failures.

The reason is that the poor are a stark and constant reminder of how narrow is the line between respectability and the begging bowl, between health and sickness, between a steady job and unemployment, between a jackpot and a disaster, between home and homelessness. It is a reminder that unsettles us. If only the poor would get on with their lives and allow us to live ours.

This was the attitude of the busy 'house full' innkeeper on the first Christmas night. Census time was an opportunity to turn a quick profit, to make up for slacker times. Such an opportunity might not come again as it was impossible to know when the next census might be. The innkeeper did not wish to waste time with these Galileans in need. He was busy with his own kind, people who could pay their way and to whom he would give value for money. His guests and himself would both benefit from this mutually acceptable arrangement. In their world, there was no room for Joseph and family.

Such an attitude of mind and heart tarnishes every generation and blights our willingness to live the commandment of loving each other. Christmas is an antidote to such fear-filled prejudice. It reminds us that Jesus did not need to claim his equality with God but rather emptied himself of power, possessions and prestige to be open to love and to be loved. His birth shows that we are so loved by God that we can risk loving each other unconditionally. It is only those who accept that they are deeply loved can take such a risk. But such risking is essential if the received love is to blossom and grow. To refuse to love, to place any brother or sister outside the ambit of our love, to dismiss another as undeserving of our care, is to reject somebody for whom Jesus came and comes at Christmas. Such rejection is unworthy of any follower of Jesus at any time, but especially at Christmas.

A happy and love-filled Christmas to you.

Holy Family

Lk 2:22, 39-40

A great deal of my life has been invested in the young and in their education, not only for work but for the three R's – recreation, responsibility and relationships with others and with God. My New Year wish is that each of today's young people would grow in maturity, be filled with wisdom and have God's favour resting upon them. According to today's gospel, these three important things happened to Jesus when he returned to live at Nazareth as a teenager. I often wonder what Mary and Joseph did to help that triple good work.

To grow in maturity, the young must have freedom, freedom to choose the better option in little things as well as in the bigger things. To make such choices one needs wisdom that is both personalised and communal. Wisdom is the appreciation of the true value of oneself and of others as integral parts of God's creation. Such wisdom is caught rather than taught. It comes from sharing chat with the elders, from reflecting together on the adult way of living, from respecting what God reveals to each one, young and old. Freedom without wisdom is like the icing without the cake, sweet but brittle. Knowledge, opinion, dogma and precept abound. True wisdom is in short supply. It must be nurtured patiently, firmly and encouragingly in young hearts. God's favour is the gift of his presence to those who believe. It is accepted and made one's own in prayer, personal and shared with others.

Mary and Joseph helped in the development of maturity and wisdom in Jesus. It was not because they were special people that they did their job so well. It was because they did their ordinary job so well that they were special. Today, we celebrate the success of Mary and Joseph as parents and of Jesus as their teenage son.

Second Sunday after Christmas

John 1:1-18, Eph 1:15-18

Another New Year has stolen upon us. As life goes on, the year seems to get shorter and life itself gets more rushed and stressful. Maybe, it is that we are becoming more and more overloaded. We are bombarded with information, knowledge, news, propaganda, advertising, entertainment and noise. The battle for our interest is intense. It is easy to dissipate one's time and energy over a vast range of experience – it is only the reflected-upon experience that enriches.

Even religious experience will not deepen faith unless one takes time to make it one's own. The word of God is a privileged way to experience the basic fact that this fast moving world is God's gift to all people without exception. He has chosen to send his Son to be one of us that we may share his life forever. This awesome message is the core of today's gospel. We may be too overloaded to hear it and may have to jettison something to be able to heed it.

My New Year wish for you is the same as Paul's for the Ephesians. 'May the God of our Lord Jesus Christ, the father of glory, give you a spirit of wisdom and perception of what is revealed to bring you to full knowledge of him. May he enlighten the eyes of your mind so that you can see what hope his call holds for you.'

Epiphany
Mt 2:1-12

Change comes more quickly and more pervasively with every year that passes. It looks as if we will not have a noticeable period of serene stability in this century to help us to adapt to all the change. We are going to live with continual change. These changes affect us all deeply, especially in how we absorb our faith, grow in it, express it, live it and share it.

The core of the faith does not change but its development in the human heart, its expression in daily life and its transmission to others must change to be part of the radically-changed life circumstances of so many believers. These radical changes affect how we learn, how we decide and choose, how we spend our time and, above all, how we relate to one another and to God.

The feast of the Epiphany contrasts two responses brought about by the birth of the Messiah. Herod thought that he could put the clock back by killing the infant and that everything would go on as if nothing had changed. The wise ones from the east were more in tune with the on-going development of God's plan. The star was there beckoning them. They trusted the God who had called them and ventured into the new world and found God.

Epiphany is a thought-provoking occasion for all who have inherited the tradition of faith in Jesus. It is a reminder that some old ways of sharing faith are no longer effective, that the people of today need witnesses rather than preachers, that the young need the experience of faith joyfully accepted and enrichingly lived to assure them of God's presence in their world. Will they find such a witness in each of us or will they follow another star to a different Bethlehem?

Baptism of the Lord

Mk 1:7-11

A key to understanding and appreciating the core sacraments in the Christian tradition is to realise that Jesus accepted the central ritual traditions of his own Jewish people and gave them a new meaning and a profoundly deeper reality.

The more obvious one was when he used the Passover feast to give his disciples the gift of his body and blood and he continues that gift for us in the transformed Passover which we call the eucharist or the Mass.

In his time also, a common ritual for expressing sorrow for sin and conversion to God was to be immersed in the waters of the Jordan. To be baptised meant simply to be immersed. However, when Jesus sent the disciples to preach to all nations and to baptise them in the name of the Father, Son and Holy Spirit, he was empowering them to do much more. They were enabled to bring all who were baptised into the familial, personal relationship with God which we call grace.

Obviously, this was not what happened when Jesus was baptised by John. Jesus did not need conversion as he already and always shared fully in the divine nature with the Father and the Spirit. What happened at the Jordan on that day was that Jesus identified with the human race of which he was truly a member and undertook to take our sins away by commitment to the Father's will. The veil on his divinity was lifted briefly and his role as beloved Son was glimpsed as the Spirit was revealed in a new way in the person of Jesus. This is our faith.

Today is a reminder that by our baptism we are privileged children of the father, touched by the Spirit, who are always in need of continuing conversion through the power and the love of God.

Ash Wednesday

Mt 6:1-6, 16-18

The talk was of overweight and exercise, of smoking and heart attacks. The tone was pessimistic. One wondered was there anything left that one could enjoy and that would be good for one. The same pessimistic approach often surrounds Lent. So much so that it is hard to believe that Lent is a preparation for the victory of Easter. The victory is Christ's and ours. It is a victory over death, sin and selfishness. Lent is to prepare to celebrate that victory.

How do we prepare for any celebration? We ensure that it will be an occasion of unity and community, that old sores will be forgiven and healed, divisions bridged, that the open hand of friendship will be offered and accepted rather than the clenched fist of intransigence, that the outsider will be welcomed as a member of the family, that many less important things will be left to one side to have time for the key preparations, that lesser celebrations will be recalled and failures left behind, that the personality of the centre-stage star will be duly honoured.

So Lent is a time of reconciliation, of sharing and caring, of making time for Christ in prayer. It is an invitation to grow closer to the one who has freed us from selfishness and made us members of his family. It is a time to deepen appreciation of our privileged greatness. Lent is meant to be enjoyed rather than endured. One could love Lent.

First Sunday of Lent
Mk 1:12-15

Today's gospel opens dramatically with the Spirit driving Jesus out into the desert. There are overtones or undertones that he must not have been keen to go. It seems strange that the Spirit of God should have been pushing Jesus to do something. It is Mark's way of highlighting the task that Jesus was about to undertake and the preparation that it needed. He was getting ready to take on the world with its subtle allurements and its enticing false promises. He was coming to offer the world the gift of God's kingdom, indeed, the gift of God himself. But it was too crowded, too entrenched in selfishness, too blind to appreciate what was offered. So there was need to repent and make room for God.

To help the world do this, Jesus needed to prepare himself. He needed the forty days. The need is the same in every age, for each generation, for every one of us, individually and as a people. We call our forty days Lent.

Second Sunday of Lent

Mk 9:2-10

Standing over an open grave, I often wonder what it will be like when we rise from the dead. Will we take up with our friends where we left off? Will we remember love and friendship? How different will it really be?

As we read in today's gospel, when Peter, James and John came down from Mount Tabor, Christ ordered them to tell no one what had happened up there until he was risen from the dead. They had seen a glimpse of his glory but no one had ever risen from the dead before so they were left wondering what such a thing could mean. We in our time are left wondering too but for us there is one crucial difference. We believe that Jesus Christ did rise from the dead and by that resurrection he guarantees our future life. We wonder about how it will happen but the fact of its happening is central in our faith. All we know is that we shall see God face to face as he really is and then everything else will fall into place accordingly. That is our hope as well as our faith. It must necessarily influence all we say and do. Keeping in mind each day that we will spend eternity with God, will colour our attitudes and our actions. Knowing that wealth will not carry weight before God will restrain our avarice. Realising that in his eyes all men and women are equal will limit our pride. The belief that love of God and of neighbour is all that survives death, will keep us from selfishness and sin.

Let us thank God for our faith in Christ's resurrection and in our own. May we meet in God.

Third Sunday of Lent

Jn 2:13-25

A trader trying to make a few pounds out of the crowd attending a match, may well view Sunday trading very differently from many others who work regular hours on a steady wage. Similarly, the traders and money changers who had gradually inched their way into more strategic and lucrative pitches within the Temple in Jerusalem, were probably horrified when Jesus lost his cool and drove them out. He must surely have seemed unreasonable and to have lacked understanding of their need to turn a shekel or two. After all, they were providing a service while the pilgrims were around.

Why did he drive them out anyway? He did it because he realised that precious things must be protected and for him, the Temple as the focus of God's presence among the people, was precious beyond price. If precious things are not protected, they gradually and rapidly wither and die, often unnoticed.

Each person, each family, each community needs to realise and acknowledge what is precious for them and to protect it accordingly. Trust is a cornerstone of human relationships. Little deceits and self-protective lies can inch their way in and pollute the inner sanctuary of trust. They must be driven out if friendship is to survive.

The ability to love and to be loved is God's most precious gift to human kind. It must be protected by absolute fidelity. God remains faithful unflinchingly. We are made in his image. Our call to imitate him is precious beyond price. Lent is an invitation to reflect on what is truly precious to us and becoming aware of our apparently reasonable compromises, to banish them through Christ's power.

Fourth Sunday of Lent

Jn 3:14-21

Some people set out to earn love. Others respond to love. The former are on a wild goose chase. The latter recognise their privilege as children of God. As Jesus says to Nicodemus in today's gospel, God loved the world so much that he gave his only Son, not to condemn the world but so that through him it might be saved.

To be saved is to be loved by God and to believe it in the core of one's heart. The human temptation is to resist being truly loved because if we really risk accepting love, God's or another person's, our shell of self-centred achievement is shattered and the focus of life moves outwards to others. This brings a peace that the selfish can never even glimpse.

The security of being loved by God is the springboard for heroism and is the source of all joy. Not to experience love is to be stunted for life. Love does not force its way into one's heart. One chooses to accept it. Accepting God's love transforms one's spirit, enabling one to love and to be loved in the fullness of one's humanity.

The fruits of love are peace, patience, strength, courage, generosity and joy. The core of our faith is that God loved us first through Jesus Christ. That is what makes each one of us special, very special.

Fifth Sunday of Lent

Jn 12:20-30

When we had our own Taoiseach from Cork, some people needed to meet him on his visits home. Many knew there was a contact man who would arrange such a meeting without any bother. In today's gospel, Andrew seems to have fulfilled the contact man's role for Jesus. There were some Greeks in town for a festival who had heard of Jesus and wanted to meet him. Being foreigners, they approached Phillip who spoke their own language. He knew that Andrew, Peter's younger brother, was the one who could put them in contact with Jesus. He knew Jesus's mind on things and his plans.

Such contact persons are needed more than ever today. There are people who have heard a lot about Jesus and the gospel but who want somebody who actually knows him in faith to lead them to him. The need is for somebody to start them off on the road of reflective prayer based on the scriptures. It is a sure way to meet Jesus. Admittedly, like the Greeks, we may learn things that are hard, but very much worthwhile.

As today's gospel has it, the grain of wheat must die if it is to bear a rich harvest. Similarly, it is through the failure of the cross on Calvary that Christ saves us. The radical message for us is that like Jesus we will have to sacrifice selfishness, security, success, popularity, power and wealth, if God's work is to be done through us.

At present, the cry of many hearts, especially among the young, is that of the Greek festival goers: 'Sir, we would like to see Jesus.' Who will be Andrew for them in our time?

Passion Sunday

Mk 14:1-15, 47

The idea of Jesus going up to Jerusalem takes on a fuller meaning when it is realised that this Holy City is 3,000 feet above sea level, on a par with Ireland's highest peaks.

A majestic setting for a fortified city that is the focus of the Jewish belief that God will be always with them to protect them, it is a city of history permeated by hope. The dormant smouldering hope was that a leader, a prophet, a man of God, a Messiah would come among the Jews to bring new freedom. His coming to Jerusalem was to be a key moment in establishing the new era of God's presence among his people. Such was the deepest longing of the Jews.

It was in an atmosphere tinged with such a longing that Jesus entered Jerusalem on that first Palm Sunday. The welcome, though fickle and short-lived, was sincere at the time. The people wanted a saviour so much. The miracle-worker from Nazareth seemed the best hope of a better future. They looked for instant panaceas. His plans did not match their short-term selfish ones. Within a week, they were easily wooed to reject him, switching their allegiance to Barabbas, leading to the crucifixion of Jesus.

This pattern has been repeated again and again in world history, as well as in our own individual lives. Today is an opportunity to come into contact with the power of the Passion and so to be transformed from competitiveness to compassion, from fickleness to fidelity, from anxiety about the future to awe about the present, with its security of God's unconditional love. Such transformation is the scenario for the week ahead, so that we do not settle for victory palms on Sunday with nails to crucify each other during the week.

Good Friday

Jn 18:1 – 19:42

We live in times when savage brutality and violent death are part and parcel of our everyday news diet. The danger is that we are no longer horrified by the horrific and we are becoming immune to the sordid. The repetitiveness of outrage inoculates us through a sense of helplessness, and lasting feelings of revulsion or pity no longer well up within us.

Something similar can happen to us religiously. The passion of Christ has been retold so often and re-enacted so frequently that familiarity can blind us to the wonder that the one who suffers is God and the one for whom it is endured is you and I. Good Friday is a reminder of this reality. It is a reality that we crowd out of our lives because the consequences are too far reaching. It is a guarantee of hope. We are not helpless in the face of death. The power of God is at work in our world. He will always be with us as we strive to build a better world.

One cannot enter fully into the passion of Christ and remain unchanged. The passion will always awaken a loving response. It is a response that can be nurtured or stifled. The choice is personal.

'By your cross and resurrection, you have set us free. You are the Saviour of the world.'

Holy Saturday

Mk 16:1-7

Many a man has chosen to die for a good cause. Fathers have died trying to rescue their children. Patriots have sacrificed themselves for the nation they belonged to. Missionaries have given their lives in martyrdom to bring the faith to the world. Jesus Christ was crucified to open for us the way to God. What makes his death different?

It is different because it was not final. It was really a new beginning. Unlike any other hero, Christ claimed that he would rise from the dead and he did. That is the foundation stone. It is the crunch question of our faith. One either believes that Christ rose from the dead and is the Son of God as he claimed, or else one rejects the lot. Resurrection is the focus of our hopes. It is also decisive in our life style. If Christ is what he claims to be, then one must accept the consequences. Either he is God or he is not. There can be no wavering at Easter. The invitation is to commit oneself to him and accept all his teachings. There is no room for compromise with him. One cannot pussy-foot with the Risen Christ.

Easter Sunday

Jn 20:1-9

The morning rain swirled around Killarney. At the foot of Mangerton, I could hardly see the outline of even this familiar mountain but the trail was well marked out by the feet of the many who have trodden this popular route to the summit.

Later, the rain stopped and the mist lifted. Then in the brilliant sunlight the grandeur of the mountains and the beauty of the lakes were visible to all. The reality had not changed. What had changed was the way I saw it and experienced it.

Sometimes, I think of God's love as being like Mangerton – solid, unchanging, eternal, dependable. It is always there but, in the troubled mists of everyday life, I do not always see it. There is a well-proven trail to guide me, the trail of prayer, service and forgiveness. It was Jesus who blazed the trail.

It brought him not only to death but to resurrection, to sharing fully in the Father's glory. His resurrection is the beacon light that beckons me onwards. It encourages me to stay on the trail, to live in hope of glimpsing the beauty of God's love in this life and of experiencing it constantly in the next life.

Jesus has passed through the mists of death to prepare the way for us. Not only that, he walks with us on our journey as one who has been through it all, to give us the confidence to believe that we are made for true greatness, God's love seen dimly now and radiantly hereafter.

'We believe in the resurrection of the body and life everlasting.'

Happy Easter.

Second Sunday of Easter

Jn 20:19-31

Laying down conditions seems to be part of human selfishness. It certainly absorbs a great deal of time and energy. One of the superpowers offers to dismantle some nuclear weapons if, but only if, the other does something similar. A trade union promises better quality productivity if, but only if, there is more money in return. An employer offers a better working environment on condition that there is less time wasted on the job. The list is endless. Few are big enough to do what is best without any conditions attached. Often friends bargain with each other though it may be done more surreptitiously. Such bargaining can rule the roost in families and even undermine our relationship with God. Sometimes it can block the reception of God's gifts as we see in today's gospel.

Thomas is the culprit. He lays down the conditions under which he will accept that Jesus is risen. What is on the cards for him is a faith experience of the Risen Lord and Thomas concentrates on the conditions under which he will accept such a blessing. His bargaining mentality almost prevents him receiving the greatest gift of all. Something similar can happen to anyone of us in our friendships, our love and in our relationship with God. A bargaining mentality can be a cancer that kills our ability and willingness to love God and be loved by him just as it can destroy our human love. Despite his 'unless' conditions, Thomas did meet the Risen Lord. Meeting him is the unconditional invitation to each of us in today's eucharist.

Third Sunday of Easter

Lk 24:35-48

Just as the disciples were frightened and disillusioned after the crucifixion, they were filled with confusion and joy after the resurrection. It was all happening too quickly for them. The women at the tomb had met Jesus. He had appeared to Peter. Now, as we hear in today's gospel, the disciples who had met him on the road to Emmaus were reporting back to the infant Church, when he appeared again.

Their joy at his presence was tangible. Their confusion was understandable. It was only Easter Sunday night and their experience of the crucifixion was still vividly imprinted in their hearts. So Jesus set about explaining once more how the Father's plan for the salvation of the world was being accomplished by his suffering as he had always foretold.

It is a message that can only be accepted through faith, a gift which God freely gives to those who are willing to accept it. It is forced on nobody. It is a gift for which all who receive it must give thanks by nurturing it in one another and by sharing it with those who have not yet received it. It is a gift which is enriched by being shared. Indeed, it is only by being shared that it can be retained.

So the command of Jesus today is that each one must be a witness to him, testifying to his death and resurrection and to the love of God at work in our lives.

Fourth Sunday of Easter
Jn 10:11-18

Even though there was a great stretch in the evening, some were anxious to be on the road home. They were sheep-men from the hill farms in the north and their lambing season was just peaking. They spoke of twins, triplets, quads and percentages. It was business talk and their livelihood. But there was more. There was commitment to a way of life, care for what had been entrusted to them by God and by the generations who had gone before them. While another might stand in for a day caring for their sheep, they themselves knew their ewes best and would share the joy of successful labour as well as helping those in trouble. Their life was to be shepherds to their own flock.

Their committed care reminded me again of why in Hebrew lore one of the most powerful images for God is that of the shepherd.

For the Hebrews, the shepherd was the leader, the protector and the nourisher. He knew the best route to travel, how to avoid danger, and where to find food and drink. As well, he would lay down his life for the flock, if needs be.

In today's gospel, Jesus takes the title to himself in regard to the whole human family entrusted to him by the Father. It was a role he lived to the full even to death.

In continuing the work of Jesus on earth, the Church in turn gives that title to those who are called to servant leadership among the people of God. So on Good Shepherd Sunday, the Church prays especially for those whose vocation it is to lead God's people in his ways, to protect them from selfish fear and nourish them with the good news and the experience of the Father's love.

The need for such faith-filled, caring commitment was never greater. We pray that many new hearts will heed the call in our time and continue the work of Jesus.

Fifth Sunday of Easter

Jn 15:1-8

It is the time of the year when every week brings a noticeable change in the world of nature around us. Branches that were barren up to recently, are now bedecked with buds bursting outwards with new leaves, new life, new hope of flower and fruit. The varied shades of green add excitement to the environment. Almost every branch has a different hue. Of course, some branches have not come to life at all. These are the ones that were broken off during the storms and so are cut off from the source of new sap, the source of life.

It is this powerful image of the vine and its branches that Jesus uses in today's gospel to teach that it is only when we are linked into him that we can achieve anything of lasting value. It is only when his life permeates our hearts that we can reach our true potential as members of the one caring family.

We cut ourselves off from him through sin, selfishness or just plain carelessness. A neglected friendship falters quickly. However, for us there is always hope. Unlike the vine branches, our rift from him can always be healed. He is always ready and willing to link with us again through prayer and reconciliation. He is the vine but he is much more. He is our saviour.

Sixth Sunday of Easter

Jn 15:9-17

Widowed at an early age and left with a young family, Brigid made a decision. She would devote her life to her children. To provide for them and to rear them was a full-time task. Often the going was hard and lonely but she never regretted the decision she had made. She found a deep personal fulfilment in giving of herself. Her giving was a giving in love. Such a giving brings a peace that the self-centred can never know.

To be a loving giver is to be truly human. We are made in the image of God, the giver of all. His Son freely decided to give himself in life and in death for each of us. He invites us to follow his example. 'Love one another as I have loved you. A man can have no greater love than to lay down his life for his friends.'

It demands faith and confidence in oneself and in God to accept the invitation. Today's gospel puts the issue plainly before us.

The Ascension of the Lord
Mk 16:15-20

Wonder-working evokes ambivalent attitudes in some people. There is an attitude that if only they had been present at the miracles of Jesus, they would never have doubted afterwards or, indeed, would never have sinned again. They would have become instant and permanent saints. On the other hand, when reports of faith healings circulate, these same people can be amongst the most sceptical about their genuineness. Why would God act so specially in such a place for these particular people? It is a question to which we do not have an answer. But if the good God healed the sick during his time on earth, it seems eminently reasonable that he should empower some of his disciples to continue that work in his Church and among his people after his death. Certainly, such power seems to have been a parting gift as he ascended into heaven.

On that occasion as well as the gifts, he set out the task of bringing the gospel to the whole world in every generation. This privileged challenge is put before all of us. Obviously, a generation before us took the task seriously enough to enable us to share this faith. Will we be less dedicated in discharging our duty? This is a question posed by the Ascension gospel.

Seventh Sunday of Easter

Jn 17:11-19

There is a longing for justice and peace on every side, justice between peoples, peace in our personal relationships. Each human relationship is a tapestry of characters and characteristics, of experiences and expectation, of feelings and fears, of perceptions and prejudices, of loneliness and love.

But a key underlying factor in the ethos of every relationship is the level of trust which permeates it. Trust is built on truth. Without truth, there is no trust and without trust, there can be no everlasting unity, commitment, service or love.

In today's gospel, Jesus prays to the Father to consecrate his chosen ones in the truth, the truth about God and about his plans for us, a truth not only to be known and spoken but a truth to be lived. He was binding the disciples into a community of believers, a Church which would make his message present to the world. A cornerstone of such a grouping had to be complete truth.

The prayer of Jesus for us today is the same, namely that we would grow in the knowledge of the truth and live accordingly. There are endless excuses for compromising the truth. To so compromise can become such a way of life that it seems to be unavoidable or even acceptable.

Upholding the truth is lonely and painful. We need to build families and communities where truth is appreciated, protected, nurtured and where each person of truth is strengthened to live the call of Jesus. We become what we do. Those who talk the truth, grow in truth. Those who speak untruth become people of the lie. We must choose which way we wish to grow. For followers of Jesus the choice is obvious.

Pentecost

Jn 15:26-27; 16:12-15

Fear, hopelesness, anger and apathy stalk the land. Fear rises in many of the sick and the old as they wonder will anybody care for them in the months ahead. Hopelessness grows in many young hearts who cannot see where they will ever find work. Anger is deep in the deprived, the poor, the redundant who see the rich get richer. Apathy leads to more widespread dependency on alcohol and drugs as the easiest way to cope. What joy could the coming of the Holy Spirit at Pentecost have for such a beleaguered people? How could today's liturgy have any relevance for real life?

Well, there are similarities with the first Pentecost. Palestine at the time was oppressed and worse was coming with the destruction of Jerusalem. There seemed to be no hope politically, economically or even religiously. Peter and the others must have longed to be back in the old days of a few years before when they had very little, but were secure in their humdrum lives. But there was no going back. Instead the Spirit of God came upon them and from being frightened, self-centred cowards, they became people of hope and courage ready to step out and build a better world for all God's people.

The first steps seemed insignificant but they were sowing the seeds of faith in Jesus as our risen Lord. From there it spread through the world and through the ages. The achievements of Francis of Assisi, Vincent de Paul, Mother Teresa and millions of followers of Christ stem from the first Pentecost.

Today's celebration is the coming of the Spirit on us, Christ's disciples of our time. Will this coming mark a new beginning in our lives? Everybody wants to change the world but few want to change themselves. Pentecost is an invitation and an opportunity to let God's Spirit change us even a little for a start.

Trinity Sunday
Mt 28:16-20

Different aspects of the character of Jesus surface at various times in the gospels. He is seen as the son of Mary in Nazareth and at Cana. At the grave of Lazarus as at Capernaum, he is the miracle worker. Gethsemane and Calvary evoke images of the suffering servant. These facets of his personality and life form an extraordinary rainbow but underlying all these elements is his relationship with the Father. It is this relationship that reveals our God to us. Again and again, Jesus reminds us by word and action of the close bond between himself and the Father. Indeed, this intimate love between them is so power-filled and awesome that we call it the Holy Spirit of personal love between Father and Son, three persons united in love in one God.

It is to this fundamental and grace-filled mystery that we turn our minds and hearts on Trinity Sunday. Often it is easier to grasp and to understand what God does than what he is but today's feast is about savouring the inner being of God. Such savouring cannot be rushed or manipulated. It is a gift of God. We ready ourselves for the privileged experience. Our role is creative listening. We quieten mind and heart to make space for God. Nothing very apparent may happen, but what a loss it would be not to be tuned into God when he chooses to reveal his inner self to us and to lead us to even glimpse more deeply how we are made in his image.

The Body and Blood of Christ
Mk 14:12-16, 22-26

Marches, parades and processions bring many people on to the streets as participants and onlookers. Marches are often a form of protest about injustice, unemployment or taxation. People feel strongly enough about something to take to the streets to express their point of view.

Parades are usually more of a celebration. Victory parades mark sporting and political occasions. Parades like the St Patrick's day one, are an expression of pride in our heritage and in our achievements. Processions have much in common with marches and parades but they have a religious dimension as well. Anybody who walks the streets with a particular group is proclaiming publicly what they believe in or feel strongly about. It is an expression of solidarity with others who share the same point of view. It is at once an encouragement and an invitation. The encouragement is to be reassured in one's belief. The invitation is to join in its public expression.

Today, many thousands will join our Corpus Christi processions. By their presence, they are encouraging belief in Christ in the eucharist and inviting others to share that faith. At the same time all those taking part are expressing their pride in the victory of Christ over death and in the hope he gives to the world through his Body and Blood.

Second Sunday in Ordinary Time

Jn 1:35-42

For me one of the great thrills of return visits home to Cork is meeting people, especially the young, whose lives I have been privileged to touch and who in turn, have touched mine. Many are former pupils I taught, others are scouts I hiked and camped with, while more are parishioners and others with whom I was part of a praying community particularly at the time of marriage or at the bereavement of a loved one. On so many occasions, it was an enriching joy to be an instrument of God's love, pointing out his presence and suggesting ways to grow in his friendship.

In today's gospel, John the Baptist has a similar role. He points out Jesus as the Lamb of God to his youthful disciples Andrew and John, both of whom commit their lives to Jesus. Then Andrew goes immediately to share his find with the older brother, Peter and so the community of the disciples is born. The Baptist's task was to help others to recognise where God could be found and where he was calling them.

We all need Baptists in our lives as individuals and communities, to prod us to move to the greatness to which God is calling us. In turn, being a believer empowers each one of us to be a Baptist to others. Parents do it every day as they guide their children to full development and genuine happiness. But the role is not confined to parents, preachers or teachers. It is open to every friend. Indeed, to be a true friend to another will always involve helping the other person to discover his or her true destiny and to follow it with courage and generosity.

Third Sunday in Ordinary Time
Mk 1:14-20

The excellence of a top class musician is the result both of talent and of ceaseless practice. The skill of a sports star comes from natural ability linked with painstaking training. In both cases, the performer chose a clear goal to which everything else took second place. The priority aim governs the whole way of life. A vision focuses the energy and good will of the aspirant on greatness. Commitment is the core of real achievement.

In today's gospel, we find the beginning of a similar choice and commitment. This time the commitment is to a person rather than to a skill. Jesus called the first four disciples. They left all to follow him. Jesus became the priority focus of their lives.

We all need such a focus or else our lives are dissipated on money, television, alcohol, comfort or even gossip. Today's gospel is an invitation to hear God's call to launch out into new generosities, new depths of faith, prayer and service, and to trust Jesus to be with us when we haul in the nets at the end of our lives. The opportunity is to leave behind our cuteness and fears and to focus on his proffered love. What if one of the gang of four had failed to respond to him?

Just as the young are greatly enhanced when an interested adult helps them to focus their lives on music, sport or academics, so too, they need to be enabled to choose Jesus Christ and his values as a priority in their lives. Such enabling is the responsibility and privilege of parents, teachers, priests and every adult Christian, today and always.

Fourth Sunday in Ordinary Time

Mk 1:21-28

Some sport followers are expert at reading a game. They can spot where a successful move begins, where an opposition's weakness is exploited, where a subtle touch of skill turns a game. Others, like myself, tend to focus on the spectacular score, on flamboyant skill even if it is unproductive, on the glaring mistakes and the glorious successes.

The crowds that followed Jesus seemed to have divided into two similar groups. In today's gospel, there were those who focussed on the extraordinary cure of the possessed man. But the wiser, more reflective people honed in on the teaching of Jesus. For them, the emphasis was on Jesus as teacher rather than as miracle worker. He was both, of course, but it was his teaching that made the more lasting impression. Why? Because he was teaching with the authority of one who knows the truth, the truth about God, about people and about the world.

The people of that time were confused about the political, economic and religious situations of their time. They were oppressed, broken and spiritually barren. The similarities between now and then are obvious. Some of the contemporaries of Jesus heeded his teaching and allowed it to change their lifestyles. So Christianity took root. Today's gospel is a call to our generation to do the same so that Christianity in our home, parish and country may be revitalised.

Do not curse the darkness of evil. Light your candle of goodness.

Fifth Sunday in Ordinary Time
Mk 1:29-39

Today's gospel is a preacher's dream. He can focus on Peter's in-laws as well as on yours and mine or he can direct his attention to the sick whom Christ cured or to the demons he sent packing. Pushed a little, the preacher could develop the disciples' hopes that Christ would cash in on his popularity because everybody was looking for him.

For me it is a different sentence from this gospel that keeps ringing in my ears. 'In the morning, long before dawn, Jesus got up and left the house and went off to a lonely place and prayed there.' If Jesus needed to set aside time to be alone in prayer with the Father, how much more do I need to do just that?

'Lord, so many things claim our attention and preoccupy us – our work or the lack of it, our security or its elusiveness, our wants that we turn into needs, our recreations that only distract us, our anxieties about our weaknesses. From all these help us to turn aside to be alone with you sometimes each day. Lord teach us to pray.'

Sixth Sunday in Ordinary Time
Mk 1:40-45

Success brings its own problems. The famous have no privacy. The wealthy live in fear of being kidnapped. The powerful are open to attack from the more powerful and from the oppressed. Many who are not famous, wealthy or powerful fantasise that they would risk the accompanying inconveniences just to enjoy fame, wealth or power even for a little while.

As we read in today's gospel, success kept Jesus out of the towns lest he be mobbed. Fame had come to him rapidly as news spread that he was working miracles. Healing leprosy caused particular excitement. As well as being an illness, leprosy made one a social outcast. A leper did not belong, had no hope of being accepted as a person, 'had to stay outside in places where nobody lived.' Indeed, anyone who had contact with a leper was ostracised as well. Yet, Jesus 'moved with compassion,' 'embraced the leper' who was then healed. Jesus risked his own security in heeding the needy one's plea.

Today, the homeless, the handicapped, the hungry, the lonely, the sick, the fearful plead with society, 'If you want to, you can help.' Will we, like Jesus, reply 'Of course, I want to' and then, like him, risk our own comfort to do it?

Seventh Sunday in Ordinary Time
Mk 2:1-12

When we are offended, a frequent temptation for all of us is to insist that the offender earn forgiveness. To make that demand is to destroy forgiveness itself. Like love, forgiveness can never be earned. It is not the stamp of approval once a fine has been paid. It is a gift and an act of love. It stems from the goodness of the forgiver, whose love evokes a renewal of friendship and commitment in the person forgiven.

What makes God God is that his love is unchanging. The only thing that changes is our response. He loves us constantly, no matter how we fail. Our choice is to respond or not to his ever-present forgiveness. It is his forgiveness that evokes our sorrow and growth in his friendship. One is sorry because one is forgiven rather than one is forgiven because one is sorry. Fortunately, the initiative is God's. The response is ours.

To experience true and full forgiveness from God or man is a treasure beyond price. The paralytic in today's gospel experienced it through Christ. So can we.

Eighth Sunday in Ordinary Time
Mk 2:18-22

Some white people in privileged positions are convinced that the old ways of white government in South Africa are best. To many of us, it seems patently obvious that every black person is as entitled to a vote as any white person. It is not so urgently obvious to us that every person in our country is entitled to a decent place to live whether they be educated or not, healthy or invalided, employed or redundant. The root cause of the blindness is the same in both cases. We tend not to see things that make demands on us and that ask us to change our privileged positions. Change is always painful for some but development is essential to keep in touch with a world that is continually evolving as a result of human discovery and creativity.

No aspect of life is immune to change, least of all religion. Religion is the expression of human friendship with God. As the human situation changes religion must change or become incapable of linking the people of our time with God. Only God and his teaching remain unchanging but the temptation is to stay with the old ways that served another generation well. There is a security in staying with what we know rather than risking following what the spirit of God is asking now. Every follower of Christ is asked to be a risk taker, to risk all for – Christ especially our certainties. In rapidly changing times, it would be amazing if what served well a century ago was still the best way to do things today.

Few travel to Australia by steam ship nowadays. This generation has developed new ways of travel. Similarly each generation must always be developing suitable ways of relating with God, of hearing his message, of applying it to the changed circumstances of its time. It is a task that must not be shirked or we risk losing the whole generation formed by the global village culture. Bemoaning the changes, or even the genuine losses, is no substitute for new evangelisation.

Jesus met similar reluctance to change among the religious people of his day. The Messiah had come but they failed to recognise him. Jesus pointed out again and again that profound changes demand radical responses, 'new wine, fresh wine skins.' Today's faith needs to be expressed in today's language and lived in today's world. It is the only world we have. This is a challenge for each one of us who follow Jesus.

Ninth Sunday in Ordinary Time
Mk 2:23 – 3:6

It is sometimes said that we are a nation of begrudgers, a people who readily belittle the other person's success or goodness. If this is true, then, we are not unlike the people of the time of Jesus who found some fault with every good deed that he did. In today's gospel, it is the healing of the withered hand. The whingers complained that it was healed on the wrong day! What an inept response in the face of sheer power-filled goodness.

It is so easy to see the small mindedness of the knockers in this case. It is not so easy to recognise the same attitude in ourselves when we wonder aloud in feigned innocence either about the motivation of the person who is caring for an ageing neighbour or about the intention of the one who gives hours of service to the community. We often shy away from acknowledging that it could be generosity inspired by Christian love that keeps them going.

The reason for our small mindedness may be that we could never visualise such generosity in ourselves so we belittle it in others to protect our self image. Such an attitude is a recipe for mediocrity, if not worse, in any follower of Jesus.

Tenth Sunday

Mk 3:20-35

Like the water we drink, some gospel values are so obvious that we ignore them until pollution hits. Then it is often very difficult to restore what has been lost. Again and again, Christ taught us that unity among people is a cornerstone of his gospel. As we read in today's gospel, he pointed out that any group of people divided among themselves can never achieve success. This is true of families, of communities, of nations, even of the Church itself. Division is the direct opposite of Christianity.

So the forces of evil make progress by setting whites against blacks, teenagers against parents, neighbours against neighbours, workers against management, sport followers against sport followers, settled against travellers, students against authorities. The seeds of evil are distrust and discord leading to destruction and death. The Christian calling is to heal such rifts, to bring the alienated together, to tear down the walls of hostility, to build bridges of reconciliation, to lay the foundation stones of harmony some place.

Christ assures us that anyone who builds unity and peace in these ways is closer to him than even his own mother and family. It is a strong way to put it, but Christ meant it.

Eleventh Sunday
Mk 4:26-34

The arrival of a new season's strawberries always interests me. As a young lad I earned pocket money picking strawberries so I had a vested interest in the health of the crop. Unlike the sturdy apple tree, the strawberry plants look fragile and yet, year after year, they produce a precious and delicate fruit. More fascinatingly still, they propagate themselves so simply. Young flimsy runners shoot out from the plant. While still nurtured by the older plant, these runners take root and in a year or two, they are producing an excellent crop themselves.

Christians are like strawberry plants. The fruit of our lives must be forgiveness, peace, care and love: precious and fragile qualities in our society. Our faith must inspire such a crop each and every day. Nurtured by an adult faith-filled life-style, the young must be enabled to put down roots in their own world and then to produce their harvest of Christ-like living.

The Bible often uses the images of seeds and crops to illustrate the nature of the faith growing within us.

Twelfth Sunday

Mk 4:35-41

News of further job losses evokes deep anxiety in many hearts. Those with jobs fear that they may lose them. The unemployed see every other job loss as lessening their own chances of being re-employed. For the young school leavers and their parents, this anxiety becomes a cancer that erodes confidence and self respect. It is a frightening situation. Many fear that we will be engulfed by the crisis. Followers of Christ could be forgiven for making their own of the anguished cry of the disciples in today's gospel. 'Master, do you not care? We are going down!'

It seems strange that the disciples should turn to Jesus for help during a storm on the Sea of Galilee. After all, they were the fishermen. They knew the angry waters and the gusting winds. Jesus was a landlubber, a tradesman from Nazareth with no touch of the sea in his veins. How could he help? Somehow, they had a glimpse of him as Lord of the wind and the sea, as Lord of all.

Today's tempest is one of powerful greed on one side with hopeless helplessness on the other. Who will calm this tempest? God will. He is not just a landlubber in the sea of economics. He is Lord of all. He challenges us to call on him, to have faith in him, to live by that faith with boundless confidence in him because he is our father.

Thirteenth Sunday

Mk 5:21-43

When a hurling game gets very one-sided, the sports commentator often remarks that it would now take nothing short of a miracle to save the losing side. Occasionally, that kind of miracle happens. Some undaunted hero produces unsuspected reserves of skill and endurance and so turns the game around unexpectedly.

Something similar, and something more, happened in the life of Christ as we read in today's gospel. The daughter of Jairus was sick, indeed, dying. Only a miracle could save her. The father pleaded with Christ to turn back the tide of illness. It looked as if Christ came too late. The girl had died.

Undaunted, Christ prayed over the girl and through the hidden power of God living in him, he performed his miracle and restored the girl to life. Even though it benefited only one little girl, God used this miracle as a sign that Christ was truly his Son.

In our time, the game of life seems very one-sided – selfishness and evil look all set to triumph. It will take a miracle to turn things around. Each of us is called to work our own miracle, a little miracle of love and service. It may only benefit one lonely person, one member of my family, one invalid, one traveller, one neighbour or one famine victim, but it will be a sign that Christ still lives in us who are his followers. Each of us is called to produce reserves of compassionate care so that hope and trust in God and in each other may be restored to life.

Fourteenth Sunday

Mk 6:1-6

A human temptation always with us is to fail to see God in the ordinary things in life and instead to seek him in the flamboyant, the unusual or exciting phenomenon. It happened in the time of Jesus, as we hear in today's gospel. His own townspeople could not accept that the boy who grew to manhood among them could have anything worthwhile to say, not to mind being a messenger from God and indeed, his own Son. They were blinded by familiarity.

It happens in all our lives. We fail to recognise true greatness or genuine needs in those with whom we live most closely. It is sometimes harder to give the travelling family, camped down the road, clean water than to send money to dig a well for the Sudanese. Yet, both are children of the one Father, our creator.

We may admire Simon of Cyrene helping Jesus to carry the cross and even envy his role while we are content to drive past the old lady on the roadside hitching a lift to visit her husband in hospital.

Often the longing to touch the presence of God sends us searching for visions and apparitions in faraway or nearby places while his guaranteed presence in the eucharist is ignored in local churches. The longing for excitement blinds us to the fundamental reality of the sacraments he has left us.

Where will we see God today? Where will we serve him? Will we recognise him living in those whose lives touch ours today? Will we be like the Nazarenes who would not accept one of their own as a gift from God?

Fifteenth Sunday

Mk 6:7-13

The world can be divided into two types of people, hoarders and scatterers. The former focus on long-term security, holding on to anything and everything that just might be useful. They save for the rainy day and save a little extra in case there is a drought as well. Their motto could be, 'What we have we hold.' The scatterers on the other hand live for today and let tomorrow take care of itself. Sometimes they are wasteful. Other times they are simply generous and trusting.

In every heart there is something of the hoarder and something of the scatterer. Often one predominates while worldly wisdom dictates that happiness is achieved by securing the right balance.

Today's gospel places the emphasis somewhat differently. It suggests that following Jesus is like going on a journey and the recommendation is to travel light. If we are to overcome the unclean spirit within us, the deep-rooted selfishnesses that can destroy love, we must trust. We must trust God as a caring Father and trust the neighbour as a sister or brother in Christ. To grow in such an attitude, we must be continually giving away what we do not really need and even a little more. We must be generous fools for Christ and for his kingdom. Only the foolish can love. The cute could never risk it.

Sixteenth Sunday

Mk 6:30-34

Achievement occupies a central role in all our lives. Sports fans boast about the successes of their stars as well as their own. Business people evaluate their peers on the strength of what they have actually accomplished. Children regale their parents with stories of achievements, big and small. In turn, parents recount their offsprings' exploits to anybody willing to listen. In so many ways, recognition for achievement seems to be very important.

It was certainly important for the disciples when they came back from their first mission as we hear in today's gospel. They overwhelmed Jesus with stories of all they had done. He felt it was an important opportunity to teach them that there are two kinds of achievers.

The self-centred kind see themselves as the creators of their own success. The others are happy to realise that all achievement is an exploration of the gifts that God has given to us, gifts of nature, of skill, of understanding, of perseverance and of choice.

These latter achievers grow in an understanding that the real fruit of achievement is not fame or self-esteem but rather a deepening appreciation that God's gifts far surpass all human achievement.

Indeed, some of the more precious things in life can never be achieved. Wisdom and love can never be achieved. Like wisdom, true love is always freely given and graciously received. Only the genuinely receptive heart is open to both. The self-centred achiever is blind to their wonder.

Seventeenth Sunday

Jn 6:1-15

We would never have expected God to use a world-wide pop concert to feed the hungry. The more obvious thing would have been to use the great leaders and the powerful governments. But some paralysis had prevented these from moving even the surplus food of Europe to the starving millions in Africa.

So God looked elsewhere for a prophet who would not only awaken a consciousness of our responsibility but who would create an atmosphere and a structure that evoke practical generosity in so many hearts. He used a Boomtown Rat to be his prophet. Bob Geldof is an unconventional choice, perhaps, but the crisis is now. To wait any longer on conventional solutions would mean increased hardship.

As we read in today's gospel, something similar happened in the life of Christ, but on a smaller scale. Thousands had been following him in a desert area. The crisis was that if they were sent to buy food, many might faint on the way. So Christ used a young lad's five barley scones to feed the crowd. The boy must have been very surprised that his little contribution could be so important in feeding so many.

God will always increase and multiply whatever we genuinely share with those in need. Trust him.

Eighteenth Sunday

Jn 6:24-35

In business a reliable brand name is an invaluable inheritance. A family brand name can be a bonus. Many older firms point to their record of service to successive generations as showing how dependable and satisfactory they are. Judge us by what we have done. Compare us with the more transient opposition. We are the best, they claim.

Today's gospel employs a similar tactic in establishing Jesus' credentials. God has always cared for his people. When they were under the leadership of Moses, God fed them with manna every day as we hear in the first reading. But manna lasted only for the day, Jesus promised bread that will last forever.

Jesus walked on the water whereas Moses had only walked through the parted waters. For the Jews, a prophet claiming to be greater than Moses must be claiming to be God's chosen one, the Messiah. They clearly understood that Jesus was doing just that and more. I am the Bread of Life, he says. My Father who has always cared for you, vouches for me as his Son.

The brand name of God's loving care made present in a human person is Jesus Christ.

Lord I believe. Help the little faith I have.

Nineteenth Sunday

Jn 6:41-52

If only I had met Jesus in person and been present at his miracles, it would be so much easier to believe in him and to accept what he taught. Such an attitude sometimes surfaces in my heart. Then I look at his contemporaries and see how they fared.

In a recent gospel, we saw how the 5,000 enjoyed the multiplication of the loaves. In today's gospel, we find some of these same people questioning their own experience of his power.

They feel that there must be a simple explanation. After all this man is from the family of Joseph and Mary. He cannot be a special messenger from God. The Jews did not like his message so they sought to discredit the messenger.

His message was that he was sent by the Father and was, indeed, his Son. The miracles were to prepare his contemporaries to accept him as God but these signs could never compel acceptance. Such acceptance is always a matter of free decision and of faith. They chose to reject him.

Nowadays, especially among some pious people, there is a temptation to seek visions and signs to justify or strengthen our faith. Such signs, even when they happen, are very transient.

The permanent sign of God's power and love is in the eucharist. It is only through faith that it can be accepted. Such faith is a living gift. How we live today nurtures or undermines our faith. The choice is our own.

Twentieth Sunday

Jn 6:51-58

Promises must always hold out a prospect of something above and beyond the ordinary and preferably be unique. Otherwise the strand of joyful hope that marks a promise is missing. On the other hand, if the pledged future is too rash, the matter is seen as fantasy rather than something open to fulfilment. So when Jesus promised to give us his Body and Blood, the hearers were incredulous as we read in today's gospel. Since they could not see how it could happen they decided that it would not happen. They restricted the power of God to their own limited understanding of reality. They reckoned without the awesome creativity of a God who loves each one beyond our wildest dreams. It is an arena of life that can only be glimpsed at through faith or not at all. The temptation is to retreat into our own world and accept only what we understand. The opportunity is to trust ourselves and God and allow him to open us up to wonders the human heart could never conceive.

The promise now is that all who are nourished by this bread of life will live forever. To risk all for this promise is the vocation of every follower of Jesus.

Twenty-first Sunday

Jn 6:60-69

It started in Christ's lifetime. The great preacher and miracle worker drew great crowds. He looked a winner. It was fashionable to be seen with him. Then, the tide turned. His preaching demanded faith in him as Son of God who could give himself under the form of bread. That was hard to take. Many could not or would not accept it and left him. He even wondered would his closest friends desert him.

It is a story that has been repeated again and again since Christ's time. The Church has enjoyed periods of popularity and prestige. It was the side to be on. At times, the tide turned. Persecution or suffering meant that it was only those close to Christ who remained faithful.

Our own time is one of challenge and cross-currents especially for the young. Church practice is not as fashionable as it used to be. Christ's teaching demands justice for all, care for the deprived, generosity and fidelity in relationships, faith in Jesus as Lord of all aspects of life. Some find the message and practice too hard and walk no more with him. As he says to Peter in today's gospel, he says to each one of us: 'Will you also go away?'

We can try to make our own of Peter's reply: 'To whom shall we go Lord? You have the words of eternal life.'

Twenty-second Sunday
Mk 7:1-8, 14-15, 21-23

It seems eminently reasonable that schools formerly used for white pupils in South Africa and now abandoned for years, should be available for coloured children where it would improve their poor quality facilities immediately. However, to some extreme whites this is unacceptable. So they bomb these buildings before their less fortunate neighbours can use them.

This warped attitude is frightening. It is the result of generations of white people regarding themselves as superior to their coloured neighbours and so entitled to all sorts of privileges. Over the decades, this cancerous selfishness grew more destructive.

It is easy for outsiders to condemn such harshness and even believe that we could never be so blind. But today's gospel is a stark reminder that the well-connected are always blind to the injustices that protect their privileges. Jesus directed the original reprimand to the hypocrites who rigorously imposed social and religious practices on the people while they ignored their responsibilities to God and to their fellow human beings.

The reprimand is as applicable today as then. As in any generation before us, the temptation is to rationalise our personal claim to a larger share of this world's goods while ignoring the plight of the homeless, the unemployed, the hungry, the handicapped, the refugee. Bombing is not the most virulent or the most subtle form of selfishness.

Twenty-third Sunday

Mk 7:31-37

Despite ever increasing sophistication in the means of communication, loneliness is a growing affliction. Some people resort to drugs because they have no one to listen to them. The expanding and generous service of a listening ear provided by the Samaritans seems to be ever more widely needed and utilised.

One of the main reasons for the rampant loneliness in people's hearts is the insidious individualism that pervades the cultural ethos that forms us. The individualism has twin roots – selfishness and fear. The selfishness dictates that one should always put one's own every need before even the most basic needs of anybody else. The fear paralyses even the generous with an anxiety that their reaching out may be rejected or misunderstood. Exaggerated privacy has become as destructive as greed. The result is that we are deaf to each other's deepest yearnings and in turn, deaf to the Spirit of God calling us to reach out to the lonely in our midst. Such deafness leads to dumbness, a failure to speak the word of friendship, of encouragement, of truth, the word that builds up God's family.

Today's gospel reports Jesus curing the deaf and the dumb. Each one of us has moments of deafness and dumbness. It is an opportunity to ask Jesus for a conversion of heart.

Twenty-fourth Sunday

Mk 8:27-35

The gambling world is littered with impoverished punters whose dead certainty tips lacked some key element that would have made them great winners. Peter is like them in having had moments of almost greatness and fluffing them.

He walked on the waters towards Jesus, but lost his nerve and sank. In today's gospel he does it again. He is the one person who recognises and publicly proclaims that Jesus is more than a prophet, that he is the Messiah and Son of God. However, when Jesus points out that this Messiah must suffer and die, Peter thunders in to correct such nonsense.

A God who would suffer and die for others seemed outlandish. Jesus would have to conform to what Peter would like God to be – powerful, in control, respectable and generally regarded as successful.

Peter had glimpsed the incarnate God whose free choice of each of us to share in his loving acceptance and in his unconditional forgiveness is a wonder beyond our wildest imaginations.

Secure in that choice, we are called to imitate our God in care of each other without exception. Such a challenging vocation frightens us and so we cut God down to size, a God limited by our puny ideas of generosity and forgiveness.

At Caesarea Jesus was not finished forming Peter. Neither is he finished with us. Take heart.

Twenty-fifth Sunday

Mk 9:30-37

It is reassuring to know that even the disciples whom Jesus lived with and taught were slow in coming to an understanding of his message. In today's gospel, we find them still haggling about precedence, privilege and popularity. The argument was about which of them was to have the key influence in the new kingdom.

Jesus reminds them yet again that among his friends service must be more important than power-filled prestige. Like the little child dependent on its parents, we ourselves owe all we have to God, our Father.

The appropriate response to this giftedness is service. The recurring temptation is to behave and to live as if our talents and our opportunities were of our own making for our exclusive benefit and enjoyment.

Humanly, it may be easy to serve the influential. There can be hope of quick recompense. But to serve the weak, the poor, the deprived, the rejected, generously, day in day out, demands that one shares the heart of God.

Today is an opportunity to seek such a heart, to ask that our hardened hearts be touched again so that we may experience our true greatness which lies in giving rather than in being served, in taking God at his word and risking our all for him.

Service is the road to love rather than to acclaim. We must choose which one we want.

Twenty-sixth Sunday

Mk 9:38-43, 45, 47-48

Jesus never shirked using strong images to make a point. Today's gospel gives one example. He speaks of cutting off one's right hand if needs be, in order to stay close to God. We are familiar with cases where the removal of a cancerous limb or organ saves a person's life. The operation may be serious and the loss grievous but in the overall context of the person's life it is worth the pain. Still, some do not have the courage to face it.

The image is a powerful one to alert us to reflect on our lifestyle. A diseased selfishness may be a cancer that is wrecking our relationships with one another and with God. It may be stealing, deceit, infidelity, tale bearing, a sharp tongue, abuse of alcohol, neglect of family, sharp practice at work or some other crippling sin. Cutting it out may be painful and require great courage. Jesus warns us that it is the only course open to us if we are to be saved. His grace, love and mercy will enable us to do just that, if we so choose. The choice is our own now.

Twenty-seventh Sunday
Mk 10:2-16

Only love can encompass both ideals and failures. It is at the core of human nature to strive for the ideal. The mind strives for ever-greater knowledge and skill. The heart longs for ever more perfect love. To be fully human is to yearn for the ideal of God's plan for us and to live out this yearning as fully as possible always.

For those who choose it, one such ideal is commitment to life-long marriage. It is an ideal that is not always reached in our limited human conditions and God understands that better than we do ourselves. The more subtle malaise of our time is that the ideal itself is being rubbished as not being worthy of human aspiration. This attack suggests that the committed human love of man and woman for each other should be reduced to a temporary contract of convenience, retractable even at the whim of one party.

Such a view is not new as we read in today's gospel. The pharisees claimed that the law gave a man the right to drop his wife whenever he wished. In their view, the woman had no equivalent right. When asked his opinion, Jesus pointed out that the man had no more right to divorce and marry another than had his wife. Moses or the law had no power to give such a privilege to the male. Jesus went on to highlight and reiterate the ideal of God's plan. Even in these times of rapid social change, when long-term commitment of every kind is endangered, it remains God's plan for all who marry. For followers of Jesus this commitment is enriched by God's sacramental presence.

God's ideal is not always achieved. It is only God's love that can embrace the failure as tenderly as the success. We are called to imitate such love.

Twenty-eighth Sunday

Mk 10:17-30

Greed accumulates wealth. Wealth nurtures greed. Wealth accumulation by one group or individual obviously deprives others of what they need. More insidiously, it endangers the inner peace of the accumulator. The person with much wants more. The fascination of wealth is very pervasive. It is like rising damp in a building. It needs very radical treatment if the whole person is not to be destroyed.

In today's gospel, Jesus meets one such endangered youngster. He saw that great possessions would destroy the rich young man. The option put to him was to give it all away and to follow Jesus. It was a decisive choice and he did not choose Jesus. He was the only one in the gospels who went away sad having met the master. He just could not pay the price, such was the grip riches had over him.

In our time, the lure of the good life is flaunted in a myriad of ways. Meanwhile, growing numbers have less and less to live on and little hope of employment. In this atmosphere, the temptation is very strong in each of us to grasp for more, to defend our privileges, to long for more security and luxuries, to silence in our hearts the cry of the poor, to excuse ourselves by highlighting those better off than us, to be quite defensive about what we have worked for, to be very reluctant to surrender anything. Without surrender, there can be no love.

The call of Jesus is to move the focus from ourselves to the needs of others. It is only through sharing with others that we receive him. It happens each time we give away what we think we need. It costs not less than everything.

Twenty-ninth Sunday

Mk 10:35-45

They say that behind every successful man there is an ambitious woman. Often it is the wife but sometimes it is the mother. In the case of James and John, it was the mother. She wanted her sons to be Taoiseach and Tanaiste when Jesus became king. One time she asked him herself for the jobs for her boys. Today the brothers are doing the asking themselves. They wanted the power and the glory as a path to greatness.

Christ's path is different. It is through service and suffering. He came to serve others, especially those who needed him most, the poor and the handicapped. His sufferings were for others. Though innocent himself, he carried our sinfulness. It is worth noting that the two readings before the gospel today are also used on Good Friday, a stark reminder of Christ's way to success.

Each of us wants the greatness which true happiness brings. The choice for us is between the route of money and glory longed for by the sons of Zebedee or the road of service and suffering travelled by Christ before us. The choice is ours.

Thirtieth Sunday

Mk 10:46-52

At some time or another, most people have longed for a second chance to make good a regretted mistake. It may be the harsh word spoken in panic, the lie protecting pride, the infidelity in a moment of passion, the worthless bauble stolen in haste, the vicious blow struck in a fit of anger, the drunken driving escapade in a mood of bravado. Whatever the error, the plea is the same. The longing is for a new beginning without the burden of past failure. It is like the plea of Bartimaeus in today's gospel whose heartfelt cry to the Lord, 'Let me see again' has echoed down the centuries. Whether Bartimaeus' loss was through illness or negligence, the pain was the same. He longed to see again.

Guilt is a blindness that darkens many a life. It turns us in on our limited selves rather than outwards to others and to God. It prevents us seeing God's all embracing forgiveness. It even blinds us to the new beginning our loved one may be offering us. The antidote to guilt is hope. Without trust, there can be no hope. To build trust is our greatest achievement. To enable another to trust enough again to be loved and to love is to be a co-creator of happiness with the Lord. It is to heal the darkness of despair, the darkest of all blindnesses.

Lord, help each of us to see each other as you see us and to see you as you really are.

Thirty-first Sunday

Mk 12:28-34

Each of us wants to be special to somebody. This is how we are made. The desire to be totally accepted, as we are, by another is at the core of our human personality. To be so loved is the deepest human longing. It is a longing that is never fully satisfied even by the most loving of human partners. It is only God who can love us so and he does.

Each of us is special to God in an individual personal way. This is what makes him God. With God, there is no comparing of one person with another. Each is cherished in a unique embrace.

To accept this love from God is to love him in return. In loving him, we love ourselves as he loves us, as precious beyond compare. The neighbour is caught up in this wave of reciprocal love because true love allows no divisions, no exclusions but rather extends to include all whom God has made.

So the dual commandments of today's gospel, to love God and to love the neighbour as oneself, is really a call to a deepening realisation of our privilege of being loved by God and, as we are made in his image, we are capable of genuinely loving ourselves and one another. To do this is to fulfil our destiny.

Thirty-second Sunday

Mk 12:38-44

Experience shows it. The poor are tremendously generous in sharing with those who have less than the little they have themselves. They do it without hope of return because those helped will probably always be in need.

Experience also shows that the more we have the more we want, the more we tighten our grip on what we see to be rightfully ours. It is a sobering thought that any increase in wealth makes most people more selfish rather than more generous. The only antidote to this growing disease of the grasping heart is to search out the needy again and again. It is not enough to wait for the begging bowl to come our way and to contribute when we cannot avoid it with good grace or with an easy conscience. To share with the poor is to share with Christ. It is a privilege to be sought daily.

The implication of the story of the widow's mite in today's gospel is that we are to share not only out of our surplus but out of our meagre resources. It is surprising how quickly luxuries become necessities if we are asked to live without them.

All in all, today's gospel is a challenging one. It should only be listened to by those who are prepared to hear it.

Thirty-third Sunday
Mk 13:24-32

Prolonged summer sunshine, which is a boon to the tourist industry, evokes fear of drought among dairy farmers. Increased social welfare benefits alleviate the lot of the poor but demand more in taxes from the better off. Victory for one political party means defeat for another. There are two ways of looking at most events. Today's gospel is no exception. For some, this gospel will sound like an impending and threatening judgement. Others will hear it as filled with promise and hope.

The difficulty is that we see things as we want to see them. We focus on what will affect our own personal, individual welfare just now. Today's gospel is a call to take a more realistic, more long-term and wider viewpoint, to see things as God sees them and as he intends them to be for the whole human family in the future. To be able to read the signs of the times in this way, to discern God's hand in current events, to know which option is best in God's plan, is a blessing to be sought after in faith. It is a gift of the Spirit given only in prayer. It is a gift each of us needs individually and as people. Today is an opportunity to seek it.

Our Lord Jesus Christ, Universal King

(Thirty-fourth Sunday)

Jn 18:33-37

While many people drift through life without ever deciding what they really want, some people are prepared to pay a huge price for what they believe to be worthwhile. It may be marathon runners who train faithfully for months just to complete the race. Often, people slave for years to achieve sporting or political success.

Money can be a great motivator as people toil daily in acquiring more and more and all to little purpose. In every generation, heroines and heroes spend their lives in the service of others and of God, believing this to be the road to deepest satisfaction and achievement. In each case, the person chooses a goal and is ready to make the necessary sacrifices to reach it.

Christ was such a person. He chose to obey the Father's will completely, to gather together a people committed to justice, love and peace. His calling was to be a servant and leader of this people, to be their king. An essential plank in his platform was truth.

Truth disturbs comfortable people and comforts the disturbed. The truth Christ announced was that each individual person is equally and uniquely precious before God. So among God's people, none may be disrespected, discarded, demeaned or exploited because of their limitations, their failures or their foibles. Rather the weak, the old, the poor must be especially treasured. Each one's talent is for the benefit of all.

This truth is not easily heeded. Selfishness filters our perception. Yet, today's gospel points out that it was to preach this truth that Christ came into this world and that it is our privilege to hear his voice and follow Christ as King.

St Patrick's Day
Lk 10:1-12, 17-20

It is a long way from Sliabh Mish in Antrim to Fifth Avenue in New York. It is difficult to see a link between a young exiled boy herding animals on an Ulster hillside and the extravaganza of the St Patrick's Day parade in downtown Manhattan. Yet, there is a link. Patrick brought the gospel to the Irish and the Irish brought the gospel to the world through emigration and mission. For some, the celebration of St Patrick's Day is a celebration of mythical Irishness and unreal nationalism, but for many the day is a reminder that God has called us to be a gospel people, living the good news and sharing it with the world.

For centuries, Christ's gospel, values and principles have been woven into our culture and heritage, but each new generation much choose to integrate them into its own lifestyle. For decades, the revitalised Irish missionary movement has taken the gospel from this country to each of the five continents. The young of today are challenged to continue that task while we salute the missionary heroes and heroines of our time and race.

St Patrick's Day is a time for remembering our past greatness, choosing our present lifestyle and looking forward to a future built on the values of the gospel which Patrick brought to us.

The Assumption of the Blessed Virgin Mary

Lk 1:39-44

It is a simple story but a profound one. It happens everyday but it is always unique. It is so ordinary that we may cease to wonder at it. It is an event that evokes wonder, praise, love, and joy but it is often accompanied by stress and anxiety. It is the story of a woman about to give birth to one whose life will be influenced by so many and who will touch so many more.

Today's gospel is about two women who were with child. It tells of Mary, herself carrying Jesus, going to help Elizabeth who was about to give birth to John the Baptist. The ordinariness and the wonder are all there; an unborn baby is a Son of God and a cousin who will prepare the way for his work; a young girl who believed that what God had called her to would be fulfilled.

My soul glorifies the Lord and my spirit rejoices in God, my saviour. O God, how great you are.

Mission Sunday

Mk 4:26-34

It becomes more obvious daily that the world is a global village of limited but sufficient resources, where greed in one corner leads to poverty in another, where inconsiderate pollution by some destroys the environment for all, where a local disaster can evoke a world-wide aid response, where small seeds of generosity in one country can bear fruit in many others, where we must quickly learn to live as a trusting and respect-filled community or else, risk extinction. It is by following the lifestyle of Jesus that we can avoid such annihilation.

To bring news of that salvation to all peoples in every generation is the call of every follower of Jesus. The call to some is more specialised and focussed. It is a call to leave the native land to build the kingdom of Christ among peoples who have not heard of him. It is to leave one's own people to bring the gospel to the ends of the earth. This vocation to the foreign missions has flourished among the sons and daughters of this island especially in the century that is almost over. On Mission Sunday, we salute the innumerable heroines and heroes who are enriching our missionary tradition and we support their heroism with our prayers and our finance.

What of the future? Our missionary tradition is changing. Dioceses are becoming more directly involved with people giving commitments of some years to the work. This is a fruitful innovation. But the fact remains that the work of spreading the gospel will always need the dyed-in-the-wool missionary, the one who commits his or her's whole working life to plant gospel seeds among those who have never heard of Jesus. The call to such a life is given to ordinary people who have extraordinary generosity.

All Saints

Mt 5:1-12

We are the stuff that saints are made of. That is a sobering thought and it is true. It is also true that nobody can be a saint alone. It is in relationship to family, friends, neighbours and work colleagues that we grow towards sainthood together. It is not to a lone ranger sanctity of just saving one's soul that Jesus calls us. He calls us to much more.

We are already the children of God and as such we must be committed to the care of each other without exception. In our own families we do not choose our brothers and sisters. They are given to us. By sharing the same parents we are bonded to each other in a tie that can never be fully broken. It is a bond that encourages us to share many a load and many a joy. Sharing God as Father creates even a deeper bond between us, one that can never be broken in this life or in the next. Today is a reminder of what binds us together.

The Feast of All Saints is an opportunity to strengthen each other's faith as a believing people who keep hope alive for each other as we celebrate the love that links us together and to those who have gone before us. It is a good day to pray.

The Immaculate Conception
Lk 1:26-38

The discovery of the centuries-old Derrynaflan chalice was yet another reminder of how our people have treated the Body and Blood of Jesus with great honour and respect. The preparation of such a chalice was a demanding task. The raw gold had to be refined through fire. The craftsman then patiently hammered out, little by little, slowly, painstakingly, the shape of the chalice. It was decorated by the skill of the artistic craftsman. Finally, it was ready to be the resting place of Jesus Christ.

Mary was, in a real sense, the first chalice. God-made-man rested in her womb. God himself was the craftsman who prepared her for the task. Her human nature was pure gold, preserved from all taint of sin. By the daily round of life, God fashioned her so that she was ready to become his mother, his first resting place.

We are invited to be chalices of Christ, precious resting places. Through daily routine of work and prayer, God shapes us gradually for the task. Little by little, he hammers out the selfishness and failures. Through suffering and hope, he decorates us as chalices for his Son.

We ask Mary to share her privilege with us and to make us worthy resting places for her son, Jesus Christ.

Year C

First Sunday of Advent

Lk 21:25-28, 34-36

Environment is crucial to the quality of life we can enjoy. The physical environment is endangered by polluted air and water. Unless corrective action is taken, humankind will not survive. The social environment is threatened by violence and drug abuse. The values which underpin the spiritual atmosphere in which we live are being bombarded from every side.

Integrity is scoffed at. Fidelity is presented as outdated. Honesty is seen as a handicap. Promiscuity seems acceptable. Self-sacrifice is seen as foolishness. The danger is that our hearts will be coarsened, that faith, hope and love will be crushed out of daily living, that we will settle for lower standards by living lives of selfishness, fear and despair. Such a tragedy is on our doorstep.

Advent is a call to face this danger, head on. In today's gospel, Luke alerts each of us to the need for urgent and radical action to protect our awareness of God's action in our lives. Paul's letter pleads with us to remember our dignity as children of God and to live accordingly.

Advent can be a protected time capsule, where precious seeds and seedlings of faith, hope and love are nurtured to strength and fruitfulness. It is a time to be treasured and not to be squandered.

Second Sunday of Advent

Lk 3:1-6

Life today is very challenging for the young. Advances in technology and communications as well as access to continuing education have created new opportunities world-wide for some. The better opportunities do not come cheaply or ready-made. Willingness to take risks and to make tough choices is often essential for success. Some face up to such challenges. Others do not.

What enables one person to follow his/her better option while another does not? Vision, personal and shared. Vision is what enables a person to face a challenge as an opportunity rather than a burden. The young often see those in authority as being strong on challenging them but short on inspiring a vision that they can make their own.

Today's liturgy is better balanced. In recounting the Baptist's plea to his contemporaries, Luke challenges us to make ready our hearts for God's new coming at Christmas by eradicating sin from our lives. Paul enkindles a vision within us. 'My prayer is that your love for each other may increase more and more and never stop improving your knowledge and deepening your perception so that you can always recognise what is best. This will prepare you for the perfect goodness which Jesus Christ produces in us.' Advent is a time to nourish the vision by sharing it in faith.

Third Sunday of Advent

Lk 3:10-18

It is a strange paradox that many who have most are often as unhappy as those who have little. The less well off know from experience the difficulty of surviving and sometimes they are very conscious of the need to support and help one another realising that difficulty could be theirs again tomorrow. On the other hand, accumulating more than one needs and hoarding against every possible crisis seems to destroy inner peace, to awaken selfish acquisitiveness, to heighten awareness of one's own rights rather than those of others, to seduce one into seeking happiness in getting rather than giving, to sap one's capacity to love and be loved, to cripple one's growth as a follower of Christ, to blind one to the neighbour's need and goodness.

Christ comes to cure such blindness and to enable such cripples to run again. Tomorrow's gospel tells how to prepare for his coming. 'If anyone has two coats, he must share with the one who has none and the one who has something to eat must do the same.' Can we afford to risk doing it? As followers of Christ, can we afford to risk not doing it?

Fourth Sunday of Advent

Lk 1:39-44

Sharing joy is a cornerstone of human living. Without such celebration, hope is smothered and when hope dies, there is no love. On the other hand, the bonding created by shared joy can lead to deepening friendship which sustains one in times of difficulty, pain and loss. Joy is precious. It is too precious to be confined to one heart. It needs to be experienced by people together so that the Lord, the giver of all joy, may be gratefully praised and the moments of joy stored into heart's memory as a source of future strength.

In today's gospel, we find two women sharing the joy of the miracle of new life stirring in their wombs. Both pregnancies were especially touched by wonder. Elizabeth was getting on in years. Mary was a virgin. Both their lives had been touched by God and by their friendship one for the other. They realised it and their hearts were filled with a joy that had to be celebrated together.

Our lives too, are frequently touched by God and by our interaction one with another. When such human interaction mirrors the hand of God in our daily lives, it evokes a joy that can blossom into sustaining love. To heighten an awareness of such joy is one blessing of our Eucharist. To be open to receive such a blessing is the privilege of every believer.

Christmas

Lk 2:15-20

As the year's biggest shopping spree comes to an end, the gospel call to prepare a way for the Lord can hardly be heard. But the call is clear. God will fill us with his peace if there is room in our lives for him. Today is the day to straighten the way, to be reconciled with our brother and sister, to break the shell of unforgivingness in our hearts and speak to those who have not been spoken to for a long time, to risk the rebuff of the hardened, to be a first mover in forgiveness, to be willing to say that friendship is important enough to be suffered for, to believe enough in oneself and in others so as to have the heart to start again. Today is the day to prepare for peace among us by asking and receiving forgiveness from each other. Today, God offers forgiveness unconditionally and enables us to forgive ourselves as well as others.

We must not abandon Christmas to merry making and money spinning. Christmas belongs to believers, to those who believe that Jesus Christ, Son of God, was born of the Virgin Mary to reconcile us to one another and to the Father. This is why he came. We must believe it. Christmas has been stolen from so many, young and old. The danger is that even believers will abandon their birthright and leave it to the scavengers who despoil every occasion and all treasures for their own enrichment. The core treasure of Christmas is awe-filled faith. Faith needs time and space to blossom and grow. It is easily crowded out when there is much to be done, so much that will pass away. Christmas is to make space and time for the God of our faith, who shares in our world, a world he created for us. Glory be to God in the highest, on earth peace to those who are God's friends.

Happy Christmas.

Holy Family

Lk 2:41-52

Families nowadays come in all shapes and sizes. For some, family is two happily married adults with several children growing up in a stable home that has close links with grandparents and other related families. For many, the experience is very different. It may be a nuclear family, parents and child with few, if any, other family links. It may be a single-parent family supported or not, by a network of brothers or sisters and other friends. Or it may be a family of orphaned or deserted children. The experiences are very varied. Whatever form our family experience takes, its effects on us continue to be profound throughout our lives.

This was also true for Jesus Christ, growing up in Nazareth with Mary and Joseph. What we focus on in today's feast is the gifted-ness of the relationships between members of his best known family. Each one in their own way enriched and influenced the lives of the others and made demands on them.

It would be too easy to dismiss this family as being so out of the ordinary as having nothing to say to us in our home situations. But the fact that in God's plan to make his love present in the world, family life was to play a central role. Today is our opportunity to recall the gifts of life and love we have received in family as well as adverting to the pain and loss we have experienced or inflicted there. It is a day for showing appreciation, a day for forgiveness and new beginnings. Above all, it is a day to remember that no matter what form family takes, it is one of God's principal ways of caring for us and making love possible in our hearts. Family is a precious gift that goes through many stages but must always be treasured and protected, nurtured and enjoyed, paid for and renewed.

Second Sunday after Christmas

Jn 1:1-18

Again and again our religion reminds us of our sinfulness and our unworthiness to be in God's presence let alone to be his children. So often the emphasis seems to be on our moral failures and on the need to improve. It is not surprising then, that some people, seeing no improvement in themselves or in others, lose hope of ever making the grade and, losing heart, they go the journey of life alone and opt out of the partnership with God which the pilgrimage of life is meant to be and can be.

Today's readings take a very different approach. They open up a new vision of God pitching his tent among us, choosing us to be children sharing in the glory of the Father as children should do.

The core of our faith is that God undertook to live in this fragile human nature to allow us to share in his eternal nature. 'The Word was made flesh' is so stupendous that we can hardly believe it but harder still to accept is that he did it just for you and for me, individually and uniquely. Everybody needs to be special to somebody but to be special to God is the most reassuring and wonderful fact of life and fact it is.

To enable us to believe it and to accept it, is the role of the Church and of all religious practice. Such belief is in itself a gift of God, a New Year present. It is a gift we can reject or accept.

God does not force his gift on anybody but to receive it, we must come with hearts that are not cluttered by selfishness, fear or unforgiveness but which are open to the wondrous light of God that never blinds us because it is filtered for us through a human nature similar to our own.

Epiphany
Mt 2:1-12

It was late on Saturday night. The chairs were stacked in the corner. The cups were washed in readiness for another day. The young people had tidied up before they left.

As the night passed, the talk had turned to religion as usual. Pat envied the wise men. The star had drawn them, enticed, led them and they had followed and found Jesus. Pat had got a good religious education and he knew it. Religious knowledge had been well taught in his school and he had responded. 'I was given a map, a guide to life. The highways and pitfalls were clearly pointed out. In some ways, it was like a geography lesson, being told about events and places but with little practical experience. I know about my God. I need a 'star' to stir me and to alert me to go to him and to follow him.'

I was left wondering. Who will place the living 'star' before Pat and his friends?

Baptism of the Lord
Lk 3:15-16, 21-22

Some New Year resolutions are shaky already. Many were under-taken without conviction about the good to be accomplished or the price of the commitment called for. It is too easy now to take refuge in the cliché that resolutions are made to be broken. They are not. In fact, what makes us truly human is that we are capable of making decisions and promises and of sticking faithfully to them even when the pressure is to yield to the selfish impulse in a moment of weakness. Lived out promises are the foundation of love and the nourishment of long term happiness.

Today's gospel recalls a time of key decisions in the life of Jesus. By being baptised in the Jordan by John, he undertook to redeem all sinners and to spend his life in preaching salvation. To post-pone the decision would impoverish the world. His committed response led to a new outpouring for the Spirit upon him.

In our lives, there are decision moments, opportunities when God calls us to new beginnings, renewed fidelity, deepening trust, more generous service, unconditional forgiveness. Every day offers such a decisive opportunity to many. Let us listen for the voice of the Son in whom the Father is well pleased.

Ash Wednesday

Mt 6:1-6, 16-18

To understand Lent, it is important to remember that it began as an afterthought. The first Christians celebrated Easter and the following weeks to Pentecost, as the feasts of the Risen Lord and the coming of the Holy Spirit. Then, it was realised that such a celebration needed preparation time. The original preparation time was just the last days of Holy Week, but gradually it grew to be the same length as the celebration itself. The preparation is built on instruction about God's plan of salvation so that we will better appreciate his choice of us. In our care-filled lives, Lent is a reminder that we are secure in God's love. This gift of faith in God's love is so precious and yet, we can let it die through neglect. Few people appreciate the gift of pure clean water until pollution occurs. Lent is a time to take protective action by cutting back on selfishness to prevent it polluting the fibre of our hearts. We abstain from some self-centred comfort to make room for the receiving and the giving that is love. Abstinence must be a prelude to appreciation or it is meaningless. Such appreciation of God and of each other is nurtured through faith shared in prayer together and in our common concern for all people.

This Lent is an opportunity to respond to God's loving plan. It will not come again. For you, may it be filled with faith, hope and love.

First Sunday of Lent

Lk 4:1-13

Three essentials people yearn for are food, independence and affirmation. The need to nourish the body is obvious but the longing to have control over one's life and the longing to be respected as a significant individual, are also very human. Being necessary for survival, these thrusts are so strong in our hearts that any one of them can come to dominate our lives to the exclusion of core values like love and respect for others. The temptation is to give the good instinct unbridled scope and that is the mistake.

Today's gospel is a dramatised report on the struggle for dominance by these human desires in the life of Jesus. The insidious suggestion was that he would misuse divine power to turn stones into bread, exchange personal responsibility over others and tempt providence in search of fame.

Our temptations are less dramatic but they really differ little from those of Jesus in their essentials. Even with half the world hungry, we still want more than our fair share of the good things of life. We may not seek power over nations but we jealously guard our privileges in residential and recreational facilities and never woo the homeless or the travelling people to share them with us. Our need for affirmation often surfaces in our failure to speak the truth in the cause of justice and right, lest others think badly of us.

His 40 days' fast tuned Jesus to be alert to the insidiousness of these instinctual temptations. The danger now is that we are unaware of how much at risk our better personal values are. Lent is an opportunity to tone up the heart to be sensitive to the call of Jesus in their defence and nurturance.

Second Sunday of Lent

Lk 9:28-36

Some people are born deaf. In others, hearing is impaired through accident, illness or age. Then, there are those whose hearing is nearly perfect but who never listen. Listening is a decision. It is a decision to give another person one's full attention and to focus on all that is being communicated. Without listening, there can be no trust and no love. Such listening is an acquired skill. In our busy noise filled world, few are prepared to invest themselves in listening especially, to the brother and sister in need or more rarely, still, to really listen to God speaking through creation and his Church.

In today's gospel, the Father challenges not only Peter, James and John but each one of us to listen to the beloved Son. The setting was magnificently staged. Jesus had taken the trio to Mount Tabor to be with him while he listened to the Father. Impetuous Peter could not stay still and listen. He wanted to rush off building tents that nobody needed.

Something similar often happens in our human relationships as well as in our relationship with God. The temptation is to be up and doing something for the deprived when often their greater need is for somebody to listen respectfully to them. It happens in families where the conscientious parent is so stretched providing for the children that there is no time to listen. The loss is great. At other times, we can be so busy talking to God that we never really listen. Here, the loss is enormous.

To be a listener is of the essence of being Christian. Listening to a loved one or to God is at the centre of growing in maturity and grace. It is only as we really listen to each other that we can hear the voice of the beloved whom he promised to send us.

161

Third Sunday of Lent

Lk 13:1-9

Spring is a time of new beginnings. Leaves sprouting, birds mating, colours peeping out, blossoms bursting, all indicate new life. Hope is in the air. Good beginnings engender hope. It is almost as if a bountiful harvest can be foreseen. But there is many a slip between sowing good seed and harvesting a bumper crop. A late frost can arrest growth. Summer storms can wreak havoc, perhaps, even total destruction. Still, there is hope. Without hope nothing worthwhile is achieved.

Something similar happens in life and in particular, in the life of faith. Baptism, first communion, confirmation, marriage vows and ordination all speak of new beginnings pregnant with great expectations. Selfishness and sin, weakness and wanderlust, fear and fantasy, pride and prejudice can retard growth into mature faith-filled living. But no matter what the setbacks here, there comes the chance to make a fresh start.

Today's gospel is an invitation to make the most of such an opportunity with its clarion call to repent and its challenging image of the barren fig tree reminding us that we are called to go before the Lord with a bumper harvest of good works, of kindnesses to those in need, of fidelity in the face of suffering, of steadfastness in sharing faith.

Repentance is unfashionable because compromise is more accommodating. But repentance is about reality. Compromise is about fantasy. The choice is to live in the world of make believe or to allow him to revitalise the seeds of the spirit within us one more time. To be willing and able, to make a fresh start in life is God's greatest gift to us. He offers it now.

162

Fourth Sunday of Lent
Lk 15:1-3, 11-32

Good stories do not need explanation. They do need to be well presented. Then personal reflection and application will enrich the listeners. Today's gospel is one such great story. Known to the older generation as the story of the prodigal son, the younger generation term it the loving father, while many good living, settled folk may well be tempted to identify self-righteously with the elder brother. Each of these three characters highlights aspects of the human heart and of life experience. The younger son typifies a common occurrence of one taking his chance and brashly taking on the world only to come crashing down with a painful bump. In failure, some return home. Hopefully, in most families, there is a welcome home. But such a welcome is sometimes resented by those who have never kicked the traces but who have meticulously served as dependable family members.

For Jesus, the story was multi-purposed. Above all, he wanted to highlight that God our Father's mercy is always awaiting us no matter what the failure and that making mistakes is part of the tapestry of human living.

Failure repented of and forgiven has the potential to help us grow in maturity and love. It is in our weakness that God's glory is revealed.

Fifth Sunday of Lent

Jn 8:1-11

The outspoken had public opinion well organised. They were very sure of their case. They sensed victory. For too long now, this outsider had been challenging their point of view. The fate of the woman in question did not matter greatly. They could use her case to silence, if not to destroy, this just man whose lifestyle, teaching and transparent honesty was an embarrassment to the establishment.

They had trapped him. Either he must condemn her and so reinforce their position or he must side with the criminalised woman and lose all credibility as a religious leader. As we hear in today's gospel, the wise kindness of Jesus in dealing with the woman taken in adultery prevailed and is still much admired.

But the spirit of these Pharisees lives on to some degree in all our hearts. Would we have stood up against the organised bandwagon and defended the unprotected woman? Would we, at least, have tackled the discrimination and demanded that the man involved be linked to the case?

If we can answer honestly what we would have done on the day, it would tell us a lot about ourselves. Just as importantly, it would help us to avoid passing judgement on others just on the basis that they had been loudly accused and denounced by the articulate.

Only the spirit of God living in our hearts can inspire us with wisdom as well as courage, with integrity as well as compassion, with tolerance as well as respect for truth, with fidelity as well as mercy, with strength as well as gentleness. We need that Spirit today as never before.

Passion Sunday

Lk 22:14 – 23:58

Pilate's image is a poor one. He is remembered as the weak-kneed ruler who through believing that Jesus was innocent, surrendered him to the mob. The mob appears in a similar bad light. Having welcomed Jesus as the long awaited Messiah on Sunday, they were howling for his blood by Thursday.

Herod made fun of the trapped prisoner and taunted him. The chief priests and elders placed a false choice before the people, making it appear that Barrabas' release depended on Christ being condemned. Together, they sent Jesus to his death.

Pilate failed to do what he knew was right, a particularly serious crime in a person with authority. The mob was fickle and easily led as groups often are. Herod was a bully boy intimidating anyone who might have spoken up for the truth. The leaders were cute manipulators of the situation to protect their own interests.

Pilate, the mob, Herod, the leaders failed to live up to their responsibilities because they did not recognise Jesus for who he really was. The reading of the Passion and the celebration of Holy Week is an opportunity to avoid the same fate.

It is a chance to deepen faith in Jesus as the One who died to save us. It is a call to imitate his generosity and courage in every aspect of our daily lives. Like Pilate and the others, we can stifle that call.

Good Friday
Jn 18:1 – 19:42

In many ways Good Friday belongs to St. John. He had been one of the first two disciples to follow Jesus and had answered the invitation to come and see. He stayed on and was with him at Cana, Thabor, Gethsemane, and now, at Calvary. Such privilege and fidelity brought its own reward, responsibility and heartbreak.

Mary was entrusted to him as a Mother. He was to care for the bereaved widow mourning the loss of her only son, executed in the prime of life. Then, there was his own heartbreak. He saw his hero, friend, companion, scourged, parched, crowned with thorns and finally, his side pierced with a lance.

Calvary must have been a lonely and exposed place for John. Some women friends had courageously stayed to the bitter end, but those disciples who might have been expected to support him, had run for cover.

John's report of the Passion events is the core of today's Gospel. It has a mysterious power to move and heal us. To hear such heroic love unfold can cure our fears and awaken a commitment to unconditional love which is the target of every Christian life. God loved the world so much that he sent his only Son to take our sins away and lead us into everlasting joy which can begin today.

Holy Saturday

Lk 24:1-12

Mystery is difficult to explain and must really be experienced to be appreciated, like love. Easter is the focal opportunity to get in contact with the mystery of the glorious resurrection of Jesus. The contact is through faith expressed in word and symbol. The many words of the vigil ceremony recount the wonder of God's dealings with his people which climax in the resurrection of Jesus. The events detailed show the power of God exercised in caring for, challenging and guiding the chosen people. The story is well told but is even better appreciated when the symbols of water and of light, of exile and return evoke in us an awareness of life and of new life, of leadership and glory, of return and homecoming.

The risen Lord leads us into his glorious life. We are an Easter people risen from sin to share in the life of God. This is the day the Lord has made, let us rejoice and be glad.

Easter Sunday

Jn 20:1-9

It was eerie in the windowless valuables vault. Once the door was closed, it was totally dark. My eyesight was as good as ever, but without light there was no way I could appreciate any of the treasures that were all around me. Eyesight without light was useless. For the believer, faith in Christ is the light that enables one to glimpse the greatness of the treasure God's call holds for us. Without faith vision is blurred. Such faith is a gift freely offered, offered again and again each time we celebrate the death and resurrection of the Lord Jesus. This gift is not forced on anybody. On the contrary, it is strengthened and nurtured only by being accepted no matter how tentatively and hesitatingly. It is a light to which one grows accustomed which colours every aspect of life, which enables one to grow in appreciation of God's friendship, to grasp his call and to respond in total love.

The renewal of this faith is God's Easter gift to us. The light of Christ beckons us on the road to joy, the joy of being sure that we are loved by God and held safely in the palm of his hand. Christ once asked a blind man: 'What do you want me to do for you?' He replied: 'Lord make me see again.' This Easter time, Lord, remove the short-sightedness of our anxious selfishness so that we may stride into tomorrow beaconed by the light of faith in the risen Christ.

Second Sunday of Easter

Jn 20:19-31

Action is a surer guideline than word when it comes to trusting another person. Assurances of fidelity, proclamations of sincerity, even words of love can be hollow unless supported by action.

Often people who have been let down or hurt need personal experience of another's good will before they can trust again. This was certainly the case of doubting Thomas.

In his absence, the Risen Lord had visited the disciples and assured them of His new presence among them. Thomas was not impressed. He felt that the Lord had let them all down by submitting so meekly to death. He would have preferred a fighter and would have died with one.

Still hurting, he would not believe or trust again until he saw and felt the Master's hands and side. His demands were met. His response of 'My Lord and my God' was a commitment to faith and service for life.

Something similar happens in everyday living. A person is wronged or hurt by another or feels let down by God. The preacher talks of forgiveness and trust. The counsellor surfaces the pain and works towards new beginnings.But often there is an insurmountable obstacle. The wounded one longs for a fresh start but is unable to take the first step.

The unspoken plea is show me your hands and heart filled with the kindness, acceptance, mercy, joy, and generosity which will restore self-esteem, confidence, faith and hope. Then and only then, will progress be possible. .There are many hurt and doubting Thomases in our world awaiting somebody to show wounded hands reaching out to embrace. The Lord has no hands now but yours and mine. Will we reach out together today?

169

Third Sunday of Easter

Jn 21:1-19

To be let down by a friend is always painful. To be let down in a moment of real crisis can break many a friendship. To make a fresh start in friendship calls for great courage, even love itself. Peter's triple denial of Christ during the Passion must have put a great strain on the bond between them. That friendship was only saved through Christ's love for Peter.

In God's plan, it looks as if it is often those who have failed him, who are especially called to give leadership in love and service in his Church. It is as if God is constantly reminding us that the people to whom he gives authority are leaders by his choice rather than by their own merit. It is God's choice that empowers a man to teach and bless in God's name, to go daily from men to God to offer him their homage and petitions and to return from God to men bringing them his pardon and hope. It is a choice of God that demands a response from the individual and from the community.

Tomorrow, we hear of God's choice of Peter and his triple response in love.

Fourth Sunday of Easter

Jn 10: 27-30

Emigration, unemployment, redundancy, family break up, demise of small schools and hospitals, change in religious practice and many other factors have all conspired to undermine the sense of belonging that is essential to all our well being. In many hearts, there is a growing sense of alienation that leads to despair and hopelessness and even, to suicide. Jesus speaks again and again of us as those who belong to him, to whom he will give eternal life and who will never be lost. It is a reassuring and revitalising message. The difficulty is to believe it and to live accordingly.

A core ingredient for growing into such faith, is to experience belonging to a community of believers who support each other in practical ways as well as sharing prayer and praise of God. Without such an experience of genuine secure belonging, faith in a caring God is almost impossible today. So the young move elsewhere. The challenge for all followers of Jesus is to build such caring, faithfilled neighbourhoods and parishes, centred on the Eucharist, celebrated and live out. To this task, some dedicate their lives fulltime as sisters, brothers and priests. Their role in forming community and gathering the people around the table of the Eucharist is a central one. Vocations' Sunday is a day of prayer that such leaders in the faith will never be found wanting. The need for them was never greater. The demands never more intimidating, opportunities never better, rewards never more worthwhile.

'Lord, inspire young men and women to give their lives to building your kingdom on earth.'

Fifth Sunday of Easter

Jn 13:31-35

Newspaper people are very conscious of deadlines. Printing and distribution schedules impose a discipline of finalising which story is to get priority on the front page. All stories are not equal. Similarly, every teacher and pupil knows that approaching examinations focus the mind and heart very decisively. One cannot cover every option. The core topics must be highlighted.

Such deadline consciousness is heightened even more dramatically for the criminal on death row. He is to die next day. Final messages take on a crucial importance. Such is the background to the current Sunday gospel readings. In today's brief extract from the core message of Jesus to the disciples on the night before he died, there is a command and a promise. The command is to love one another as he has loved us. The guarantee is that we will truly be disciples if we do so. There is both a challenge and a reassurance.

To love as Jesus loved is to strive to recognise God present in everyone we meet and to treat them accordingly. Seeing each other as made in God's image is the cornerstone of forgiveness, and without forgiveness there is no love.

The words of Jesus are unequivocal. Be generous, nurture no grudges, truly love and allow oneself to be love and all will be well. If only we would trust him and trust our better selves.

Sixth Sunday of Easter

Jn 14:23-29

Crisis is always unsettling. It leads either to barren defensiveness or new relationships. In time of change, one temptation is to cling to securities that previously channelled life but are now barren. Such clinging can be treacherous because the former fruitfulness of the old ways can prevent us seeing the new realities, challenges and opportunities. This was a real temptation for the first disciples of Jesus especially those closest to him. They had enjoyed and been enriched by the years of deepening personal friendship with Jesus. Then came the passion, death and resurrection and finally ascension. The human camaraderie was no more but Jesus was offering a new intimate form of presence and friendship. The Paraclete would initiate it in their hearts.

It was not easy for them to make the transition. It called for faith in Jesus as God rather than experience of Jesus as man. It was only the spirit who could take them over this chasm and then only if they really wanted it.

One choice is to be like the establishment at the time of Jesus who stayed with the barren certainties of the old religion and thus missed out on the Messiah. The alternative is to accept the promise of Jesus to send an advocate to teach us all things and to form us as heralds of the gospel. It is a disturbing but worthwhile prospect. There is no middle ground.

The Ascension of the Lord

Lk 24:46-53

Witnesses usually achieve fame or notoriety only when the events they have experienced lead to a conflict of evidence in court or before a tribunal. Then, the query arises whether the persons in question know anything really significant and whether they are speaking in an objective and truthful way. Opposing legal eagles often discredit witnesses on one or another score, perhaps drawing from other aspects of their life style to intimidate the fearful but honest persons. In court, the best witness is often quite objective and is not personally involved in the outcome of the case. It was somewhat different when Jesus sent the disciples out as witnesses to his life, message and resurrection. He was sending them into a world more searching and dismissive than any court or tribunal. But they were not merely reliable reporters of the past but were to be people whose own lives had been radically changed by the good news which they were recounting.

It is such committed witnesses that the world and the church need today. A heresy of our time is neutrality about values. Jesus was far from neutral about truth, justice, creaturehood, forgiveness and charity. Neither can his followers be neutral. Each one, alone and together, is promised power from on high to enable us to be courageous witnesses to the gospel by how we live and how we speak.

This is today's message.

174

Seventh Sunday of Easter

Jn 17:20-26

The content of Sunday gospels is varied. Some give glimpses of key events in the life of Jesus. Others give aspects of his teaching. Today's gospel is part of the prayer of Jesus for the disciples and for all those people who through their preaching, would come to believe in him in the church. The prayer is a prayer for unity, a prayer that the unity among believers would resemble the complete unity between Jesus and his Father. The unity between Father and Son is the ideal towards which all human unity and love strives.

It is in the family that such relationships begin, survive, grow and bear fruit. This is what makes the family so precious. It is made to the image of God himself whose core is unchanging love between Father and Son and Spirit and which overflows into love for all the human race. The family mirrors this divine nature when its members commit themselves to each other forever in generosity and joy and in turn, are enabled to reach out to others in concerned service. Such a twofold witness is a sign to the world of God's presence. It is the sign that our time needs so badly.

Pentecost

Jn 14:15-16, 23-26

For some families a wedding anniversary celebration is a great focus of thanks, joy, reconciliation and hope. We remember the day when in love and trust, two people started a new family committed forever to care for each other and for their children. We look forward to that life continuing in the extended family with relationships nurtured by the love expressed and shared at the celebration. If any family member refuses to turn up for the celebration, there is always great loss on both sides.

For the Church, Pentecost is both an anniversary and a birthday. At Pentecost, the Spirit of God's love focussed on Christ's disciples to bind them together as a people committed to establish his kingdom on Earth. It was the birth of the Church. But Pentecost now is also like a wedding anniversary. It is a celebration of the spirit of God's love bringing us together in worship of God and care of each other. It is a reminder that the spirit has always been with the Church guiding, healing, helping, challenging and making it holy. Pentecost looks forward, calling us to commit ourselves again to the shared responsibility of enabling all God's people to serve him.

In the family, the roles of parent, child, grandparent differ from each other but complement each other. In the church, there is a similar variety of roles but all are essential. In our time, the role of leader is particularly crucial. As never before, perhaps, our leaders are called to courage, wisdom, understanding and love. At this Pentecost, as each of us commits himself or herself again to the family which is our Church, let us pray especially for those called to leadership that God may transform them with his spirit so that we may all come closer to Jesus through his Church whose birthday we celebrate.

Trinity Sunday

Jn 16:12-15

Somewhere I was taught that a mystery is something that cannot be explained and that one cannot fully understand. That is true but it is less than half the truth. Many of the the most precious things in life cannot be completely explained, they can only be experienced and appreciated. Take for example trust, forgiveness, loyalty, friendship and love. Each of them is hard to define but when we meet them in life, we know they are real. They are mysteries. God is also a mystery. He cannot be fully understood. But we can grow in appreciation of his love.

He has made himself known to us as Father, Son and Holy Spirit, and in the name of that Trinity we ask his blessing on all we say and do. It is the name badge that expreses our faith. It is our way of glimpsing at the nature of God. God as Father is not merely our creator, but also, the all-caring Dad as Jesus called him. God as Son helps us to appreciate that just as he came to share fully in human nature as Son of Mary, we, humans, share in the nature of God. The Spirit is God present within us and among us as a powerful love that transforms our lives.

To have faith in the Trinity is a gift of God. Today we say thanks for that gift and ask that we may become more aware daily of God's presence in our lives.

The Body and Blood of Christ

Lk 9:11-17

A visitor was due from abroad. He was to be met at the airport. How would he be recognised? Hardly by his clothes, his hairstyle or his baggage. It would be better to agree on something that would clearly distinguish him from many others. Maybe, it would be safer to have two signs of identification.

After the resurrection, when Jesus joined the two disciples on the road to Emmaus, they did not recognise him until he broke bread with them to ease their hunger and to strengthen their faith. Things have not changed.

The world recognises Christ's followers in the breaking of bread both in the feeding and care of the deprived as well as in the breaking of bread at the eucharist. These twin badges show clearly who we are. Both are essential to our identity as followers of Jesus.

To celebrate eucharist without practical concern for the needs of the deprived is to make mockery of our Christian calling. To spend oneself in the service of the poor without the nourishment of the eucharist is to be impoverished in the midst of God's bounty.

Neither identification has a priority over the other. They go hand in hand, nourishing our faith and proclaiming to the world that Christ is truly risen and lives on in his followers who are the Church. To share in such an identity is our privilege and our joy.

Second Sunday in Ordinary Time
Jn 2:1-12

Sensitivity to the real needs of another person is a key strand in the ability to relate to people and to grow in love. Even generosity is often counter productive when sensitivity is missing. Dedication is no substitute for understanding. Fidelity without insight is barren.

Of course, sensitivity without the decisive unselfishness that leads to appropriate action is as useless as a football team without the ball. There will be no worthwhile goals achieved. The ability to spot a neighbour's needs and the willingness to meet them as best one can, is a precious gift that enriches the human family beyond measure.

It is a gift we see in Mary in today's gospel. She seems to have been one of the first to realise that when Jesus brought the disciples with him to the wedding at Cana, the wine supplies were bound to be over stretched. Mary lost no time on excuses or explanations. The bride and groom would be very embarrassed by suggestions of meanness.

Unable to help much herself, she trusted that her Son could save the day and she challenged him to do so. He may have been less than pleased to be asked just then, but he rose to the occasion.

Something similar often happens in our lives. A Mary of some kind spots the need and invites us coaxingly to help. The choice for us then is to resist the enticement to generosity and thus, gradually to kill what is best within us or alternatively, to be sensitised to another's need and so grow in the qualities that makes us worthy to be children of God and brothers and sisters of each other.

Third Sunday in Ordinary Time
Lk 1: 1-4, 4:14-21

Pity Christ. He had made just the front page of the Capernaum Examiner. At least, his name was on everyone's lips as a miracle worker and as a great preacher. He went back home to Nazareth. The locals would accept his miracles but not his preaching. Wasn't he one of their own? How could he have anything important to say to them? Didn't they know as much as he? Sure, his parents weren't educated either! They could not hear because they knew Christ so long.

Has your husband or wife been trying to tell you something important and you have not heard because you know him or her so long? It is amazing how the truth can come to us. It comes through a child, a parent, a friend, a neighbour, a colleague on the job. Truth comes from God. God's messenger may be so ordinary and so well known that we ignore his message unwittingly. To hear the truth, to listen to it, to take it to heart can be difficult but it is an essential step on the road to happiness and to God.

Fourth Sunday in Ordinary Time

Lk 4:21-30

The grievance was a genuine one and the mood of the meeting was angry. Each succeeding speaker fuelled the seething emotion with calls for hardline action. Joe took the microphone and began to speak. The hall hushed. There was something about him that arrested one's attention. He spoke calmly and simply, pointing out a more just and reasonable way of doing things. Many heeded him and were nodding in agreement. But the more aggressive were hellbent on militant action no matter what the majority opinion was. The heckling started. His motives were questioned. What was he getting out of settling? What could you expect from a person of his breeding? Who was he to tell anybody else what was right and should be done?

His integrity was obvious and his argument irrefutable so some resorted to slander, ridicule and mob rule. He was shouted down.

This happened to Jesus when he spoke at home in the synagogue at Nazareth. It has happened often since to many a man or woman speaking the truth with courage and love. Do not be surprised when it happens to you.

Fifth Sunday in Ordinary Time
Lk 5:1-11

Fish and fishermen are continually in the news as countries tussle for an acceptable way of rationing out the harvest of the sea. I have heard fishermen say that catching a fish is easy enough. It is finding the fish to catch that's causing the problems. It seems that things were no different in Simon Peter's time. Together with his companions Peter spent the whole night fishing but with no results. Then suddenly almost from the shore, Jesus, the carpenter's son, the landlubber from Nazareth directs the fishermen's attention to a shoal of fish in the deep water. They were truly amazed. Obviously, Jesus would be a great addition to any fishing crew. But, instead of joining the fleet, he invites Peter, James and John to leave their fishing and to join him working full-time establishing God's kingdom on earth. It was not that their fishing was not worthwhile but God asked them to undertake another job. What made that job important was that is was what God wanted. God still invites us to work at the job of spreading the gospel, each one in our own unique way. None of us must neglect the opportunity given to us. The need for fulltime volunteers who leave all for the sake of the gospel is as great now as it was in Simon Peter's time.

Sixth Sunday in Ordinary Time

Lk 6:17, 20-26

Among those who will not be at the eucharist next Sunday, there are two categories for whom its gospel is particularly poignant.

Some are too poor to come. They may be ashamed of their shabby clothes or embarrassed at having nothing to put in the collection boxes inside and outside the Church. They may be old or blind or handicapped and have nobody to enable them to go. Then, there are those who are so down-trodden or oppressed by their unending struggle with deprivation and poverty that they have lost heart and so no longer desire to be part of a community that has neglected them so badly.

Others are too rich to come. They may be surrounded with security and comfort, that they no longer feel any need of God or of the praying community . They may be so busy making more money that they have lost sight of what life is for. They may have so many recreational and travel options that worship of God does not rate a mention.

For one group, the gospel has a message of hope, for the other, a dire warning . For the few, money and possessions become so infatuating that short term comfort, pleasure and power displace love, peace and joy as priorities. Such blindness gets rapidly worse and is almost irreversible. The message of hope is that despite the failure of the human race to share the good things of this world more fairly, God loves each one equally and cares for each uniquely. The challenge is to avoid setting one's heart on wealth. The surest way to prevent oneself being coarsened by money is to share it with the needy brother and sister daily and to settle for a little less when looking for one's share of the cake.

Seventh Sunday in Ordinary Time

Lk 6:27-38

Every so often, a person feels asked to do the impossible. It may be a constant challenge like the deserted mother trying to rear a family on a frugal weekly allowance or the person with the chronic debilitating disease making heroic efforts not to lose hope.

At other times, it may be a once off situation like saving somebody in a stormy sea or winning a sports event against the odds or raising huge funds for a community project during a recession.

Hopefully most people have one experience of achieving the apparently impossible or at least, the very unlikely. Such experiences should be recalled before reading today's gospel in which Jesus puts extraordinary challenges before us. Love your enemies. Give to everyone who asks of you. Do not judge others. Treat others as you would like them to treat you.

The rewards promised are enticing. But is it an unattainable pipe dream? On one's own it is. But we are not alone. Jesus is with us and sends the spirit of God to live in us, to reassure us, and to strengthen us. When we respond to the Spirit, true greatness follows. Nothing is impossible with God.

Eighth Sunday in Ordinary Time

Lk 6:39-45

The first words a child speaks always arouse excitement and interest. Proud family members share them and report them to all and sundry. The words are analysed. Reasons are offered why it was these particular words rather than others that were spoken first.

Beginning to speak is an important stage in any child's life and the words spoken reveal something of the wonder of the development of an unique human person. The words we speak link us with each other in a way that inspires or destroys, encourages or restricts, develops or retards talent, peace, friendships and hope. Today's readings remind us that a person's conversation is the acid test of character and that a person's words flow out from what fills the heart.

Each evening we would do well to listen again in our hearts to the words our lips have spoken throughout the day to alert us to what goodness is within us, what needs healing and forgiveness, what bitterness or self-centredness needs to be attended to, what bridges need to be rebuilt, what love needs to be nurtured, what peace needs to be restored. Words are rarely neutral. Our own words can be a mirror to show us what we are. God's word is a beacon to show us what we can become.

Ninth Sunday in Ordinary Time

Lk 7:1-10

Locals can sometimes cause surprise in how they treat the outsider who has come to live among them. This happened in the case of the centurion of Sunday's gospel. He had come to Capernaum as an officer of an occupying army and yet, despite that role, he had won the respect and support of the local leaders.

They put in a word with the master when the centurion's servant was dying. They were so effective that the Roman was embarrassed at the Lord's impending visit to his home. A committed Jew would never visit a Gentile house, but Jesus was prepared to do just that to help the sick man.

The centurion felt unworthy of such a privilege. Jesus was fascinated that an outsider could have such faith in him, a Jew. It could only happen in Capernaum. It certainly could not happen in Nazareth, where they ran the Lord out of town when he refused to prove himself by working wonders. In Capernaum the atmosphere of respect and faith was conducive to new faith.

Faith and love cannot be proven. We must be open to experience them so as to appreciate them. Today's invitation is to believe totally in the Lord's present care for us without having to challenge him to prove his love. For deep happiness, we need to trust all our loved ones in the same way.

Tenth Sunday

Lk 7:11-17

Some good people who have provided for themselves always, often find it very hard to accept welfare payments or even, neighbourly assistance. It goes even harder on such people to have to ask for what they need. If only somebody would notice and do what they could to help without waiting to be asked. This is what Jesus did at the gates of the city of Naim as we read in today's gospel. The widow's only son was being brought out for burial. Unannounced and uninvited, Jesus restored the young man to life and to his mother.

Many people follow that example in our society. They see a neighbour's need for a cooked meal, a babysitter, a lift to the hospital, somebody to read the paper to them, a word of encouragement, a helping hand in one way or another and they respond generously as best they can. They risk being rejected but rarely are, because a helping hand offered with deep respect and genuine love will always touch a chord in another human heart. Indeed, such a hand of friendship can evoke new hope and life as the hand of Jesus did at Naim. In today's world, a follower of Jesus cannot settle for just responding when asked for help but must create one's own opportunities for generous service each day.

Eleventh Sunday

Lk 7:36 – 8:3

At one time or another, everybody fails to live up to his or her ideals, talents or opportunities. Some fail through weakness. Others fail by choice. Some succumb to temptation because they see no other option in their circumstances. Others have many options and choose the selfish one.Their responsibility is the greater. But personal failure is a fact of every life. How we deal with failure is what makes us what we are and what we become.

Some just condemn failure, their own or preferably, another's. Condemnation can be seen as a deterrent to future misbehaviour and so is expected to protect important values. Condemnation can also crush hope and so, block any chance of a new beginning.

Mere condemnation was not Christ's way as we hear in today's gospel where the woman who had a bad name around the town washed his feet with her tears and covered them with kisses and ointment. His starting point was love for the one who failed so that forgiveness could lead to a new and better way of living. His approach was a courageous one because condemnation is always more acceptable to the selfrighteous ones. It might seem that he was approving of the evil whereas he was focussing on the core precious goodness of the woman who had sinned. He always did that, loved so unconditionally that the people he met were enabled to make a fresh start. He invites us to do the same always.

Twelfth Sunday

Lk 9:18-24

We seem to be complex creatures. Personal happiness and fulfilment is a priority on our life agenda. Our first instinct is to grasp the easy option and settle for immediate joy. But life teaches that long-term happiness does not come through grasping but rather through giving, that we are made to be generous sharers as well as grateful recipients, that love demands a willing ability to give as well as to get and we are all made for love. This lesson is not easily learnt because the instinct to selfishness continues to be vibrant in us all. It is an instinct that destroys justice, the foundation of all peace. It is an instinct that is nurtured by self comfort and convenience. To prevent that instinct destroying us, Jesus challenges us in today's gospel to refuse it daily nurturance and, instead, to choose to pay the cost of inner peace by taking up the cross of self-denial everyday and following him. It is the only way love can blossom.

We are made for love based on gratitude, justice, service and hope. Self-denial makes room for these to flourish in our lives.

Thirteenth Sunday

Lk 9:51-62

Heroes and heroines arouse interest and awe in our hearts. They may be volunteers for the Sudan and Ethiopia, or human rights activists in China and Central America, or missionaries stretching from Pakistan to Peru. Somehow, in some way, they hear an inner call within themselves to give their all in a very radical way for the service of their brothers and sisters, hungry for sustenance of body and spirit.

In today's gospel, we hear of one such radical call. Jesus invited the young man to come with him and to do it now. The young man agreed to come, but later. Putting it off, placing conditions on his response, destroyed the young man's opportunity of the greatness which is knowing Jesus Christ and serving him in the neighbour.

Do we ever postpone the call to be generous with our time or talent? Do we agree to follow Jesus but only on condition that our comforts and privileges are safeguarded? Do we hedge our bets so well that we never really choose Christ? These are today's gospel questions.

Fourteenth Sunday

Lk 10:1-12, 17-20

Parents give their children two valuable gifts, roots and wings. Roots include a sense of belonging to a family, a community, a tradition, with its securities, its values, its strengths and its responsibilities. Such roots ensure that young people have a sense of identity and self-worth that enables them to fulfil their commitments and choose a lifestyle that is not blown about by every fad or whim.

The gift of wings is the supportive freedom and wisdom that blossoms into the ability and willingness to leave the nest and take on a life of one's own while retaining great warmth for the home base. Giving roots demands on-going strength. Giving wings calls for pain-filled generosity.

As we hear in today's gospel, Jesus gave both roots and wings to the disciples. He rooted them in knowledge and love of the father and then, he sent them out to build up God's kingdom in the world around them.

He does the same with each of us. He nourishes our roots in prayer time and in the Eucharist and challenges us to use our freedom to build a better world wherever we are. It is a freedom some are loathe to use.

Fifteenth Sunday

Lk 10:25-37

The snag about being a Good Samaritan is that one never knows where it will end. One act of kindness can lead to another and even blossom into a relationship of caring, and caring is a risky business. It is much safer to contribute to the collection box or sponsorship card and leave it at that. After all, our taxes pay for nurses to care for the sick, social workers to rehabilitate the misfits, police to control the delinquent and so on. But that is really a very superficial argument. There is always need for the Good Samaritan who is prepared to get personally involved with the person cared for, even with the one who does not appreciate the help.

On the road to Jericho, the original Good Samaritan did not just call an ambulance or the police, he ministered to his brother in need himself personally. The need for such personal care is all around us if only we had the eyes to see the need and the heart to meet it. Faint hearts never sparkle or ignite.

True, getting involved in caring is a risky business but caring is the test of the genuineness of our faith. How many of us will pass that test this good Samaritan week-end?

192

Sixteenth Sunday

Lk 10:38-42

Christ was lucky in his friends. In the midst of the hustle and bustle of a wandering preacher's busy life, he had a haven. When the going was tough he slipped away occasionally to the home of Lazarus, Martha and Mary, at Bethany. It was near Jerusalem and miles from home.

It was Martha who first invited him home, but it was Mary who made him feel at home. It was Mary who understood that there is more to friendship than doing things for the other person. True enough, if Martha did not get the supper ready, they would all be in trouble. But Mary was aware of the other need, the need of people to be accepted for themselves, to share the fears, the anxieties, the hopes and the joys of life with another. Each of us needs somebody to listen.

In all our caring for each other, we must do more than provide a service, important though that service may be. We must link up as people who cherish each one we serve.

In today's world the listening and accepting ear may be the greatest act of friendship.

Seventeenth Sunday
Lk 11:1-13

The first prayer that arises in many hearts is one of asking for personal needs. This is fair enough because even the Lord taught us to pray regularly for our daily bread. But prayer cannot stop there. If we are to grow in the knowledge and appreciation of our God we must move on to praise his name with grateful hearts. This is what we will do for all eternity and beginning now is a good start for eternal happiness.

Genuinely, praising another is allowing oneself to recognise unselfishly the goodness of the other person and being inwardly touched by that very goodness. Expressing such praise brings great joy and uplifts the praising heart. Such prayer is the core of deepening faith. We strive for it in the 'Our Father' when we pray 'Hallowed be thy name.'

Petition is a prelude to praise as an awareness of our needs leads us to rejoice in our God who meets these needs. Petition and praise are joined in today's gospel.

Eighteenth Sunday

Lk 12:13-21

The beach was a hive of activity. Among the younger children there was an air of competition about the building of forts in the sand. Each group of youngsters wanted to build better than anybody else. Even in the heat, they worked hard and long. Their achievements were really something to admire. But the tide turned and was gradually creeping shorewards. It nibbled at the outer fortifications and then quite rapidly the entire array crumbled.

Something similar often happens in life. People may spend years building for themselves little kingdoms of wealth, power, influence or popularity. Then the tide of health or good fortune turns and suddenly or gradually, all is swept away like the sandcastles on the beach. It is a stark reminder that we have not here a lasting city. It is a reminder that we need constantly because the temptation is to imitate the youngsters in the sand and spend our energies trying to be better than our neighbour by having more wages, better holidays, nicer things, a bigger car, higher status or greater influence, whereas the most lasting achievement in life is what we do to benefit others. Giving brings more lasting happiness than getting.

Christ has another way of putting this message today.

Nineteenth Sunday

Lk 12:32-48

Success in life seems to arise from the gift of spotting a worthwhile opportunity as well as the willing ability to exploit it. In short, a player spots an opponent's defensive weakness and pounces to make the most of it, and so, a star is born.

In business, the shrewd operator sees the need for a product and quickly fills in the gap, and so, fortunes are made. In Christian living, the alert follower of Jesus is tuned to every opening for prayer and service and responds generously, and so, saints are made daily.

Some never see the frequent opportunities that come their way to create happiness among us. Others lack the courage to take their chances to do so, sitting back awaiting the really perfect opportunities and life passes them by. The reality is that we can block out God's call and gradually deaden it almost completely, or alternatively, we can respond in little ways each day and so become attuned to the Spirit of God living within us and among us.

Today's gospel is a clarion call to stand ready because God's call comes in situations that we may never suspect or expect. To miss his daily calls is to be deprived in our everyday living. To be tuned to creation and to the Creator is the path to happiness.

Twentieth Sunday

Lk 12:49-53

Christ knew where he stood. He fully realised that evil, selfishness, fear and sin were part of the world of his time. He was not so foolish as to think that everybody was going to agree with his teaching and so build a world of peace based on justice and love. But he was very clear that that was exactly what his followers must work towards in every situation in every generation no matter what the cost.

Such a task is bound to cause division, division between those who want to build a society where care of one another is the life-blood and those who want a society where might is right and self-ishness is the touchstone of action. Those who aim to live by Christ's values must risk unpopularity and rejection even among those closest to them. You cannot expect everybody to agree with you when you do what is right. To always do what one knows is right, is often a lonely road. Christ asks his followers to travel that road and not to compromise on fidelity or justice. He calls them to generosity and courage. Some answer such calls. Some do not. So there is bound to be division, two against three and three against two as we read in today's gospel.

Twenty-first Sunday
Lk 13:22-30

Television has taken us inside high profile sporting events in ways undreamt of a generation ago. At Croke Park, Landsdowne Road, Portmarnock and the Curragh, the telescopic lens zooms in on the VIP section. There are the people selected for reasons of power or prestige, of service or office, or privilege or influence, whose prime seats are specially reserved for them whenever they choose to arrive. Elsewhere, the general crowd may struggle for a view or not get it at all. Such is life.

In contrast, today's gospel tells us that in God's kingdom in this life and the next, there are no such favourites. Indeed, those to whom most has been given may be most at risk. In God's plan, faith and opportunity are pure gift, given and calling for an active response. It is not enough to have been blessed with the name of Christian. Our daily lives must be permeated with the spirit of Jesus, a spirit that is constantly taking the initiative in forgiveness and reconciliation, in compassion and caring, in friendship and fidelity, in enabling and encouraging, in patience and peace building.

It is a spirit that is nourished by prayer, lifestyle and eucharist.

Twenty-second Sunday
Lk 14:1, 7-14

One immediate reaction to today's gospel is to say that Jesus just could not be serious with his suggestion that instead of inviting to our celebrations friends and those who will invite us back in return, we should invite the poor, the crippled, the lame, and the blind. It is just not on, we feel.

The crux is that Jesus is serious. He is condemning our exclusivity, that trait within us which causes us to exclude from our circle people who will not benefit us or who, indeed, may threaten our comfort in some way.

We exclude because we are selfish or fearful. Our selfishness causes us to grasp the good things of life for ourselves no matter what the consequences for others. Such selfishness can be so habitual that it becomes unconscious and may even be misunderstood for success. Such confusion is rampant and destructive of inner peace. Our fear prevents us trusting those who differ from us socially or economically. This fear is a paralysis that inhibits even the first step in reaching out to others and so, much good is left undone.

Jesus promises to cure both our selfishness and our fear if we want him to do so now.

Twenty-third Sunday

Lk 14:25-33

They must be fooling some of the people some of the time because the advertisers continue to woo our custom with promises of free luxuries of one kind or another. Deep down we probably all realise that between us we are paying in full for every such gimmick but we seem to find payments less painful if the extraction is under some other guise like getting a barbecue through buying petrol. The ploy is to create an attitude that the advertisers' goal is what they can give us rather than what they can get from us, that they really want to leave us better off than everybody else.

In Christ's time, his followers were swept along by a wave of emotion into believing that he would set up a kingdom where they would be special and better off than the rest of the world. He quickly disillusioned them. Anyone who wanted to be a true friend of his would have to pay the price. The price was and is to care for one's neighbour as lovingly as oneself. To pay the price is the great daily challenge and cross.

The big difference between Christ and the commercial world is that Christ does really want to leave us better off through what he can give us in love and peace. The price is to remove from our hearts any selfishness that would corrode God's love, to trust him when that love seems absent, to allow him to mould us to his image, to give him our hearts. It is a price that is tiny in comparison to the reward but it must be paid.

Today's gospel is a clarion call to examine whether we are prepared to pay that price. If not, he cannot give us the greatest gift of all, his love.

Twenty-fourth Sunday

Lk 15:1-32

The ability to forgive or be forgiven is a sign of both genuine wisdom and mature love. In today's gospel story, we find a young man and his father who have both and an elder son who has neither. The wisdom is in recognising that failure does not lessen one's unique preciousness but more importantly, it creates an opportunity for another person to grow in love. The love is in seeing the person before the problem and building relationships anew before extracting apologies, settling accounts or exacting promises.

Such wisdom and love in all their fullness are found only in God and we are the beneficiaries when we open ourselves to receive his forgiveness. But we are also made in the image of God, and so, true human greatness is alive in our hearts when we mirror authentic forgiveness to one another.

What a noble privilege to glimpse the mystery which is forgiveness.

Twenty-fifth Sunday

Lk 16:1-13

Joan was a good neighbour and always had the best of intentions. She chatted to all and sundry, trading little bits of gossip. The gossip was usually true and harmless. But she was not too careful about her words. She felt that her tales were only little ones anyway. She always thought that she would never join in real character assassination. Gradually, however, and almost unnoticed, the gossip got more juicy and nobody was safe from her tongue.

It was the old story all over again. The person who is careless about little things will not be reliable in more important matters. In today's gospel, Christ puts the matter more positively. He points out that the person who can be trusted in little things is the one who can be trusted in important matters. The challenge is to examine how we measure up in the 'little things' like small lies, casual gossip, petty pilfering, paying our bills, abuse of position and so on. Care in such matters is a cornerstone of happiness. The alternative is that we may grow careless about the really important matter of our privilege as children of God.

Twenty-sixth Sunday

Lk 16:19-31

Some of Christ's stories are so familiar and seem so straightforward that we readily settle for a reasonably comfortable surface message from the story and ignore the powerful inspiration it is offering us. Today's story of Lazarus who survived on the crumbs from the rich man's table, is a good example.

The obvious message is that the wealthy should contribute more to charity and that maybe, though we do not consider ourselves as rich, even we too could be more generous. End of story so it seems.

But it is not the end. The punch line is that money with the comforts and pleasures it brings, can prevent us from even knowing our need of God. This is the greatest tragedy of all, never to allow the experience of God to touch our lives and our lifestyle.

The temptation is to put a price on everything, even on God, to feel that religious practices, contributions to charity and avoiding the excesses of sensual living will ensure salvation.

The message of today's gospel is that it is something different that is needed before all else. It is to live more simple lives less cluttered with possessions,pleasures or power so that God can fulfil his promise to do greater things for us and in us.

Life seems to show that it is easier for the poor to do this and so in the end they have the advantage like Lazarus.

Twenty-seventh Sunday

Lk 17:5-10

Today's gospel has a surprising message, a sobering warning and a pressing invitation for the committed, for those who do their duty faithfully week in, week out. Through the parable of the master and servant, the message is that fidelity does not automatically entitle one to the good things of life. Everything in this world is truly God's gift and he can give as he chooses. We cannot earn what is his to freely give. The warning is that fidelity to duty can lead to self-righteousness if we forget that it is God's grace that enables us to be faithful in the first place. The invitation is to thankfulness, thankfulness for God's every gift but especially for the gift of faith in him. It is this faith that enables us to ask God for the apparently impossible, to make us saints now, people who will build up his kingdom on earth through persevering service to the neighbour. Thankfulness to God is a foundation stone of happiness. It protects us from envy, disappointment and despair. It keeps the heart from withering and nurtures it in love. For all God's gifts, let us give thanks.

Twenty-eighth Sunday

Lk 17:11-19

It was 5 a.m. as I walked across the quiet and deserted city. The traffic lights changed and the silence was broken as the high pitched bleep-bleep sounded. This is a new device that tells blind and partially sighted people that the traffic has been stopped to enable them to cross the street in safety. There in the solitude of a sleeping city, I was again reminded of the gifts of hearing and sight that I take so much for granted. As I stepped it out to catch the early train, there was a prayer of thanksgiving in my heart, a fresh awareness of God's gift to me. The prayer of thanksgiving adds nothing to God's greatness but makes us grow in his love. Thankfulness is the cornerstone of happiness. Without gratitude there is no love and unless gratitude is expressed, there is no joy.

In Christ's time, ten lepers received the gift of new health miraculously. As we hear today, only one returned to give thanks. Are we part of the grateful minority?

Twenty-ninth Sunday

Lk 18:1-8

Jesus was a great exponent of the story and the parable to make a point, especially when it was central to his message as we find in today's gospel. The image is of a one-woman pressure group and a very formidable one she was. Bureaucracy had not dealt fairly with her in her widowhood. Indeed, those in power had ignored her. She decided on a sit-in at the judge's door until her case was heard. Her conduct was not conformist but it brought results.

Jesus suggests that we do the same with God. We should refuse to leave his presence until our prayer is heard. An intercessory prayer sit-in is recommended. The point is that we may need to show God that we are serious about him and about his care of us. When we camp at his door, he will come. Living as we do in a society of instant food and instant cures, we often expect God to take our calls instantly. We are like children who demand instant response and who drop anybody who does not meet their need for immediate attention.

God tests us more than that. He tests our perseverance and through that perseverance, we grow in his love.

Thirtieth Sunday

Lk 18:9-14

We seek it here. We seek it there. We seek security everywhere. We seek it in our health, in our work, in our relationships, in our homes and, especially, in our faith. The striving to have unshakeable foundations to the core values in our lives is as strong as the instinct for survival itself. This searching thrust is a gift of God, a route designed to lead us to God who is the source and goal of all our longings. But the security instinct can be so strong that when it seems threatened, we develop a defensive shell that prevents us growing in inner peace by letting us settle protectively for conformity rather than courage, for selfishness rather than service, for wealth rather than wisdom, for a view about our calling rather than a vision of our greatness.

This is what happened to the people in today's gospel who prided themselves on being virtuous and despised everyone else. They saw rigid faithfulness to tradition as being the answer to God's call rather than recognising his hand in the strivings and struggles of the people of their time.

To smash their shell of smugness, Christ told the parable of the Pharisee and the despised tax collector going to pray. One knew his need of God and had mercy shown him.

Thirty-first Sunday

Lk 19:1-10

People often make their own luck. Certainly some people are very willing to make the most of their opportunities, to do what they can to enrich life for themselves or for others. Then there are the knockers, who complain about another's good fortune and focus on all the reasons why such blessings are undeserved by the recipient.

People were much the same in Christ's time, as we hear in today's gospel. Zacchaeus was an opportunist. He had an eye for the quick profit and used it well. But he also had an eye for the genuine article and, when Jesus came along, he realised that there was something more valuable here. Despite his lack of height, he was determined to see Jesus. The sycamore tree gave him a vantage point. He took it. Jesus made contact. Zacchaeus was moved to change his lifestyle. Jesus went to the house of Zacchaeus for the day. The crowd did not like it and offered a thousand reasons for the host's unworthiness.

Nothing much has changed. Jesus passes by in our lives. We need to find a space, a vantage point, to meet him; to step out of the clutter of life; to find our own sycamore tree. He will make contact, live in our hearts and change the core values out of which we live. The crowd will not like it either, thinking that we are beyond change, beyond greatness. But nothing is impossible with God, as Zacchaeus learnt.

Thirty-second Sunday

Lk 20:27-38

Joe had never bothered much about death and resurrection. True enough, he had been to many funerals but they were always somebody else's. It was bonds of friendship or family ties that brought him to bury the dead. He had always quickly returned to the business of real living as he saw it and never risked thinking about death. It could make one morbid so he shirked it. Now things were different. He knew from his illness that the next funeral he would attend would be his own. He was puzzled rather than frightened. If there were nothing after death, then there was nothing to be frightened about or nothing to look forward to. Yet, he did look forward. Gradually, he realised that he really did believe in a life after death and that in fact, this belief had surreptitiously influenced all his life, his generosity, his kindness, his repentance, his fidelity and his religious practice. As death drew near, he wanted to believe in the resurrection more and more deeply. Unlike the Sadducees in today's gospel, who were searching for smart arguments to disprove resurrection, Joe was growing more and more content in the belief that the God who made him would bring him safely home to heaven. So his peace deepened and we all knew that once again God had fulfilled his promise to be close when most needed, at the hour of death.

Thirty-third Sunday

Lk 21:5-19

Fear is a very destructive force. In tough times, fear drives many a man to defend his own corner so tenaciously that he refuses to consider anybody else's interest. Oftentimes such conduct destroys worthwhile opportunities and initiatives.

In uncertain times, some people hanker for a certainty that reassures them that they are right and safe themselves while the rest are seen to be offside. It is fear of the risk involved in the search for what is best now that drives them to try to put the new wine of today's world into the old bottles of yesterday's lifestyle. It cannot be done.

The times that we live in are both tough and uncertain as were the times Jesus foresaw for his followers after his death. They would face plagues and famines, persecution and betrayal. Yet as we hear in today's gospel, he assured them that there was no need to be afraid. The antidote to fear is trust, trust in God and in his world including ourselves. He has made us for himself and died to save us. We will not easily be lost.

Christ's trust-filled followers must be in the vanguard of building a new world everyday.

Our Lord Jesus Christ, Universal King

(Thirty-fourth Sunday)

Lk 23:35-43

There is a great tussle for the minds and hearts of the young in Ireland and throughout the world. They are presented with many choices. Some woo them to total freedom and pleasure through drug dependency and licence as the road to happiness. Others suggest to them that the key to success is to grab what you can get, and that violence is an acceptable and powerful tool. Traditional leaders teach that conformity to the tried and tested ways of the elders is the only way to build a better world for themselves. The young find it hard to see it that way. They are often unsure and experiment with varied options, and many get hurt and lost in the process.

The feast of Christ the King is an opportunity to offer them the most worthwhile option of all, namely, to follow Christ as guide to true greatness through his teaching enshrined in the gospel and in the Church. He leads by his own lifestyle of service to others and respect for all. As a friend, he offers intimacy and support through prayer and eucharist.

Each of us is invited to make him King of our hearts and of our lives.

St Patrick's Day

Lk 10:1-12, 17-20

First time out, he was an emigrant, lonely beyond measure, forced to leave his family and native land. Abroad, he worked at the most menial tasks that nobody else would do if they could avoid them. He yearned for home. He turned to God in prayer at all hours of the day and night. He managed to return home. All his prayers seemed to be answered but his inner peace was short-lived.

A deep yearning was stirring within him. Despite their superiority in trading and in war, the people of his land of exile were impoverished. They had never known Jesus Christ. The inner call to bring faith to the Irish proved stronger than the longing to stay at home. He returned, still an emigrant but now a volunteer, still lonely but now motivated by love for God's people. Fearful perhaps before the hostile paganism but he was never daunted. The rigors of slavery had strengthened him for the tasks ahead. Fidelity to prayer learned as a herdsman stood him in good stead as an apostle to the Irish race. In a generation, the seeds of faith were planted throughout the land.

The harvest of Patrick's work has formed us. Many of our race are following his missionary example. Patrick's Day is theirs in a special way. It is ours too, when we nurture in each other the faith, hope and love, he brought to this island and when we share the treasure with the next generation, no matter how unwelcoming the atmosphere seems to be at times.

To be a son or daughter of St Patrick is no rallying cry for the faint-hearted or for those who easily lose hope in God. Dóchas linn Naomh Pádraig.

The Assumption of the Blessed Virgin Mary

Lk 1:39-44

Advertisers and newspaper editors are always on the look-out for a key word or phrase that will attract attention in a commercial or in a headline. Often, the attraction is in something new or unusual but the well-known and familiar can also evoke an immediate interest and response.

The gospel story of Mary's visit to Elizabeth has been told so often over the last 2,000 years that when it is read again today there may be nothing fresh to catch our attention. Yet the story is vibrant for the believer.

The incident is commonplace enough. Two pregnant women share their story of new life within them. But Mary and Elizabeth do more. They share faith in the wonder of God's choice of them. God had called them to differing and demanding roles in life. It was only his power working within them that enabled them to respond. Their meeting strengthened their faith. It enabled them to express their thanks and appreciation of God's goodness in their lives. It helped them to grow in his love. They were enriched by the sharing.

Often, we go it alone, unable to share even with those we love, our faith in God, our hopes and our fears. Maybe this feastday could be an opportunity to explore at home what God's coming means to each member of the family. As we undertake the task, may each one, like Elizabeth, be filled with the Holy Spirit.

Mission Sunday

Lk 5:1-11

Jerry's interest was greyhounds rather than religion but my arrival always provoked a discussion about Christ. Jerry argued that Christ was running with the hare and hunting with the hounds. On the one hand, he tells us 'When you give alms, your left hand must not know what your right hand is doing; your alms giving must be secret.' On the other hand, as today, he tells us 'Let your good works shine before men, that they may glorify your Father in heaven.'

Behind all that chat Jerry was well able to reconcile the two points of view. He agreed that good works should never be done just to show off. But the second admonition bothered him. He saw it as a challenge to preach Christ's values by how we live and to support our missionaries who take his message out to the world. Mission Sunday was always a tussle but most of the time Jerry was generous beyond expectation. Once, on the eve of Mission Sunday, Jerry had his shirt on a six-to-one outsider at the dog track. It won. Jerry was tempted to put the entire winnings on the plate on Sunday morning. Would you?

All Saints

Mt 5:1-12

Cork and Kerry people are regarded as the best supporters to follow a team to Thurles or Dalymount, to Croke Park or Lansdowne Road. They travel by train, by car, even by plane and a few heroes go by bicycle. Some are well organised – they travel early with all arrangements made. Others just make it. Once there, they are all united in hope. Not that they don't enjoy the journey too. There is many a helping hand, a lift to the station, a scouring of the country for tickets in case a friend would be left behind, a hand aboard with the plastic bags as the last train pulls out. A song shortens the journey. Many hopes are strengthened and anxieties halved by being shared. Those who travel early or the night before, are looking out for their own, eager for reunion, trying to reserve a place for somebody close.

Today, All Saints Day, is their day, the day of those who travelled before us. They have gone by many routes; as parent or priest, as widow or orphan, as nurse or teacher, as rich man or poor man, as young or old, as invalid or by sudden call; some heroes have gone the road of suffering.

They await reunion. Today is the day for the helping hand, the word of encouragement and forgiveness to ensure that there will be nobody missing when we reach home.

The Immaculate Conception
Lk 1:26-38

Foundations are usually buried deep in the earth and once laid, they are not open to inspection. Their worth can only be gauged by how well they sustain what is subsequently built upon them. Indeed, one criterion of the success of such preliminary work is the fact that it is taken for granted unless attention is drawn to it specifically.

Something like this happens in the gospel accounts of the life of Mary, Mother of Jesus. The first mention we have of her life is at the Annunciation. That occasion was marked by an earth-shattering invitation and an extraordinary response. The invitation was to become the Mother of God. The response was concerned and confident; concerned about her own inadequacies but confident that nothing is impossible to God. It was the event that changed not only history but God's way of relating to his people. However, it was not the beginning. Long before then, the Father had prepared Mary for this moment. The foundation he laid was that from the first moment of her conception, Mary shared in the saving grace of her future Son and so was preserved free from all taint of sin and selfishness.

It is this foundation that we focus on and honour today. It was a preparation worthy of the master builder. It is a key strand in our devotion to Mary.